Introduction to

SOCIAL WORK

A Primer

Introduction to
SOCIAL WORK
A Primer

Betty J. Piccard
School of Social Work   The Florida State University

Fourth Edition

THE DORSEY PRESS
Chicago, Illinois 60604

This book was set in Palatino by Eastern Graphics.
The editors were Leo Wiegman, Mary Lou Murphy, and Jane Lightell.
The production manager was Irene H. Sotiroff.
Malloy Lithographing, Inc. was the printer and binder.

ISBN 0-256-03679-9
Library of Congress Catalog Card No. 87–70917

Printed in the United States of America

1 2 3 4 5 6 7 8 9 0 ML 5 4 3 2 1 0 9 8

PREFACE

The fourth edition of *Introduction to Social Work: A Primer* offers a concise picture of basic issues in social work policy and practice. Designed for the first course in an undergraduate social work program, it uses a systems approach to explicate the interrelationships between theory and practice, past and present. Since the first edition in 1975, instructors in social work programs in small colleges and large universities have adopted this text and found it helpful. Students with little or no background in social work have been able to understand the profession, its values, skills, and knowledge. The first edition filled a need for a brief survey text with linkages to the professional literature. Those of us teaching the introductory course at that time knew where to find the information we needed, but it was not available in a single text. Since that first edition, with the help of faculty who have used the book, more topics have been added, while the original brief format has been maintained.

The fourth edition is divided into four parts. Part One consists of two chapters. Chapter One discusses the value and history of social welfare and social work and explores the differences between the two. Chapter Two relates these to a systems framework and explains the basic concepts of systems theory. Part Two is made up of three chapters concerned with direct and indirect service delivery to individuals, families, and small groups. Part Three addresses indirect social service delivery or working with larger systems. Part Four discusses other important concerns such as casework with special populations, the feminization of poverty, international social work, and the future of social work.

This fourth edition contains the following new information: (1) The privatization of social services under the Reagan administration and the effect of this on social workers and their clients. (2) More discussion of women's and minorities' problems and the feminization of poverty. (3) Discussion of Canadian social services as part of the international perspective.

Many instructors and colleagues have contributed to this book with careful feedback over the past ten years. I would like to thank Luke Fusco of Wilfrid Laurier University and Albert Roberts of Indiana University for their helpful critiques of this fourth edition manuscript.

Betty J. Piccard

CONTENTS

PART ONE   *Background of social work values and history* **1**

1 Social work philosophy and values **3**
Social welfare, public welfare, and social work, 4
  Questionnaire.
Knowledge, skills, values, 7
Skills, 8
Social work values, 9
Summary, 14

2 Social systems **16**
What is a system?, 16
A social work system, 18
System terms, 19
Individuals, small groups, and communities, 21
  Individuals. / Small groups. / Community.
Social work inputs: Planned change, 25
Roles for social workers, 27
Summary, 29

3 The history of social work **31**
Some systems affecting history, 31
The charity organization society, 39
State and local responsibility, 40
Mary Richmond, 42
Freud and psychiatry, 43
Differences between England and the United States, 44
Summary, 49

PART TWO   *Direct services delivery* **51**
4 **Social casework** **53**
   Initiating the planned change process, 54
   The interview, 56
   Contract, 58
   Other systems, 64
   Change models in casework, 66
   Summary, 72

5 **Social work with families** **74**
   Psychoanalytic approach, 80
   Integrative approach, 82
   Communicative-interactive approach, 83
   Summary, 85

6 **Social work with groups** **87**
   Group work models, 88
   Social goals model, 89
   Remedial model, 91
   Reciprocal model, 93
   Group work techniques, 96
   Task and growth groups, 100
   Summary, 105

PART THREE   *Social service delivery in macrosystems* **107**
7 **Social service organizations** **109**
   Public agencies, 109
   Voluntary agencies, 111
   Voluntarism, 112
   Social work in nonsocial work settings, 113
   Private practice, 114
   Professionalism, 116
      Social work education. / Ph.D. programs.

8 **Social work with communities** **119**
   History of community work, 120
   Community work models, 121
   Model A, 122
   Model B, 125
   Model C, 126
   Phases of planned change, 128

Similarities and differences, 132
Summary, 135

PART FOUR   *Some special concerns*   137
9   **Social work with minorities**   139
Direct practice, 139
Minorities and indirect practice, 146
Racism and institutional racism, 148
Feminization of poverty, 149
Summary, 150

10   **International social work**   151
Canada, 154
Great Britain, 154
Switzerland, 157
Summary, 159

11   **Some implications for the future of social work**   161
Religion, 162
Economics, 165
Politics, 165

**Appendix A   National Association of Social Workers
(NASW) Code of Ethics**   175

Appendix B   An International Code of Ethics   177

Appendix C   Three case studies   181

Selected bibliography   189

Index   i

PART ONE

Background of social work values and history

Part One will attempt a kind of framework for the study of social work and social welfare. Some definitions of commonly used but less commonly understood terms will be suggested.

A simple explanation of social systems theory seems in order, to provide an orientation for examining ideas, concepts, and theories in an orderly fashion. Again, some definitions and some examples will be provided.

A knowledge of the history of social work and its relation to other historical events seems imperative in order to put social work into a reasonable perspective.

1

SOCIAL WORK PHILOSOPHY AND VALUES

The terms *social welfare, public welfare,* and *social work* require some defining. Wilensky and Lebeaux, in *Industrial Society and Social Welfare,* have defined social welfare in two ways: as residual and institutional.

> Two conceptions of social welfare seem to be dominant in the United States today: the *residual* and the *institutional.* The first holds that social welfare institutions should come into play only when the normal structures of supply, the family and the market break down. The second, in contrast, sees the welfare services as normal, "first line" functions of modern industrial society. These are the concepts around which drives for more or less welfare service tend to focus. Not surprisingly, they derive from the ethos of the society in which they are found. They represent a compromise between the values of economic individualism and free enterprise on the one hand, and security, equality, and humanitarianism on the other. They are rather explicit among both social welfare professionals and the lay public.[1]

The first conception describes institutions that come into play only when normal structures such as the family and the job market break down. The second sees welfare as a normal function of modern society. For our purpose, we may accept the second conception as social welfare and the first as public welfare.

Most people have no trouble accepting the concept of need on a temporary basis. Food stamps, aid to families with dependent children, medicare, and medicaid can be seen as desirable and necessary emergency measures. Most people do have trouble seeing these

3

measures as a way of life. When they become institutionalized, they are somehow less acceptable despite the fact that some of the population is in dire need of them. Thus, residual tends to mean temporary or emergency.

Wilensky and Lebeaux suggest that very few institutionalized services exist in the United States today.[2] One example of such service is the public school (which is not usually considered welfare). Public education is available to all, regardless of their need or inability to pay. These authors identify such services as free hospitalization and free medical care as needed, but admit they are not available in this country, except as residual, means-tested services.

Wilensky and Lebeaux wrote their text in 1965. In 1987, the ethos of society in the United States, as in Canada and other developed countries, is slowly but surely becoming more concerned about economic individualism and free enterprise, and less concerned about humanitarianism. The result is that public welfare under any definition has become less popular than in 1965. Governments at every level—local, state, and federal—are not only making cutbacks in the services offered, but are trying to rationalize these cutbacks. Conventional wisdom holds that an improved economy precludes the necessity for expanding or even maintaining public welfare programs. If people must, they will manage.

Social welfare, public welfare, and social work

Social welfare involves all the functions performed by society to meet the needs of all the people in the society. Institutions such as schools, highways, and post offices are included, as well as social security, public assistance, and health insurance.

Public welfare is the system that supplies certain goods and services to certain people whose normal sources of supply have broken down. Families without a wage earner, the aged and aging, and the handicapped are examples of people who might be unable to meet their own needs. Government support for Lockheed and Chrysler in the past few years has benefited the rich more than the poor. The federal government saved both these major industries from economic disaster through huge government subsidies. Though rationalized as "trickle down" measures, these have not been called welfare.

With such simple, rational definitions, how can there be so many and such strong feelings about the whole concept of welfare? The answer is that rational definitions do not determine feelings. An interesting experiment is to ask families, friends, or casual acquaintances for a brief rational explanation of the terms in question.

Richard Titmuss, noted British economist, is one authority who suggests that public welfare ought not to be differentiated from social welfare. He suggests that the two are the same. Programs, whether public or private, which are designed for the welfare of any group benefit other groups as well. In his view, most of the money spent in public welfare is spent on middle- or upper-class people. If we look at public programs in the United States, we see that the Veterans Administration and social security programs are tax-funded programs, most of whose provisions benefit groups other than the very poor. Furthermore, we must recognize that various types of tax breaks involving great sums of money are available only to the very rich.

For the most part, social work as a profession, and social workers as individuals, tend to agree with Titmuss and to see welfare as an all-inclusive function of society today. While many social workers are involved with the residual aspects of meeting emergency situations by providing goods and services where there has been a breakdown, many others work as planners, educators, and administrators concerned with the broader aspect of welfare.

Social workers might see tax breaks for the wealthy as less worthwhile uses of public funds, but they subscribe to the proposition that public support for any given group has an effect on all groups. If there is only a limited amount to be spent, it should be spent for those whose need is greatest. Social workers see the importance of looking at large complex systems, trying to see the relationships between systems, and of planning for the best use of goods and resources.

For many people in our society, the word *welfare* has strong emotional connotations. To a recipient of public assistance, "the welfare" may be seen as an all-powerful monolithic organization wielding life and death power. To a taxpayer struggling to keep up with increasing living costs, welfare may mean "no-good deadbeats getting something for nothing." To a semanticist, the word may mean simply faring well, a state of well-being. It is clear that neat, tidy definitions do not adequately explain the kinds of conflicts that may be elicited by any mention of social welfare or public welfare.

QUESTIONNAIRE

Answering the following questionnaire may give you some idea of where you stand with respect to the residual-institutional dichotomy, as well as an idea about your attitudes toward welfare and social workers. Do you agree or disagree with the following statements?

1. Welfare recipients are mainly people who are too lazy to work.
2. Illegitimacy is encouraged by the practice of increasing the amount of the grant according to the number of children.
3. Receiving public assistance runs in the family.
4. Welfare recipients receive all necessary medical care free of charge.
5. Social workers should be very careful not to pamper applicants for public assistance.
6. Most social work is done by psychiatric social workers.
7. Mentally ill people are nearly always best cared for in mental institutions.
8. The trend in the treatment of juvenile delinquency is toward more permissiveness.
9. A social worker's main job is giving people advice.
10. The idea of helping people to help themselves assumes a degree of competence in welfare recipients that most do not have.
11. The use of groups by social workers is a fad that will probably die out soon.
12. If you had a serious problem, you would probably think of asking for help from a psychiatrist rather than a social worker.
13. Policemen cannot use social work methods because they deal with a different type of person.
14. If a person under the influence of alcohol asks for help, a social worker should always refer him or her to another agency.
15. If a person admits using drugs, a social worker should always refer him or her to the police.
16. Persons who are having marital problems would probably rather talk with a psychologist than with a social worker.
17. To say that a social worker helps people to help themselves means that he or she knows what is best for them and helps them to get it.

18. Social workers should work without pay for the satisfaction of helping others.

These questions, your answers, and discussions around them may help to clarify some basic issues and facts in social work. On the other hand, the questionnaire may serve to pose new questions and cloud some issues previously perceived as clear. Over a period of several centuries, entire populations have wrestled with the questions of rights and responsibilities of individuals and groups, of communities and political institutions.

Knowledge, skills, values

Harriett Bartlett, in her article "Social Work Practice" in the *Encyclopedia of Social Work,* says:

> Social work practice is recognized by a constellation of value, purpose, knowledge, and interventive techniques. Some social work practice shows more extensive use of one or the other of the components, but it is a social work practice only when they are all present to some degree.[3]

These attributes are necessary for a social worker, then: knowledge, skills, purpose, and values.

Bartlett, in her book *The Common Base of Social Work Practice,* describes the problems involved in differentiating between values and knowledge. She suggests that *values* are what is regarded as good and desirable while *knowledge* refers to verifiable experience—as objective as possible. Together, these two determine and guide the skills. Bartlett says, "The oldest and most widely held value in social work asserts the worth and dignity of every human being. Of increasing importance in social work thinking is another value that has been expressed variously as self-determination, self-fulfillment or self-realization."[4]

Knowledge of human behavior has developed rapidly in the last 70 years. We recognize now—since Freud's initial work—that many factors affect an individual, and that even more factors affect groups and communities. Human development from birth to death is an important facet of the knowledge we need, but it is only one facet. The old argument about the influence of heredity versus environment requires broadening and deepening.[5] It is impossible to predict future behavior simply by a knowledge of genetic, prenatal, infantile, and early childhood history. We think that an individual begins life as a unique being whose family, growth pattern, and other stimuli have some effect, but we are no longer likely to predict a simple cause-effect relationship no matter how much we know about an individual's past.

We know, too, that people behave differently in their own families than they do with their friends; differently with strangers; and still differently in large organizations and in communities. Social work skills have developed as we have gained knowledge about different kinds of behavior in different kinds of settings.

Somewhat belatedly we have come to recognize that people from minority social, ethnic, and cultural backgrounds react differently when they relate with people and situations from the majority culture. We have learned that the majority view of our society is not the only one, or even necessarily the best one. The term *institutional racism* refers to one form of social inconsistency, inequity, and injustice with which we have had to become familiar and knowledgeable.

Knowledge of how larger systems affect individuals and families is also part of social work. Politics and the economy have broad influences on welfare policy, and therefore on the ways that society deals with problems. Personal problems and public policy are inextricably related, as we shall see as we learn more about the history of social work and social welfare.

Skills

Baer and Fedrico, in their work *Educating the Baccalaureate Social Worker,* define *skill* as "the ability to perform actions based on knowledge, experience and aptitude".[6] They go on to list ten competencies required for beginning level practitioners and then to break these down further to more specific activities. Clearly, skills are interwoven with knowledge and values.

Casework skills have developed as a result of our efforts to help individuals as individuals on a one-to-one basis, using either a problem-solving[7] or a psychosocial approach.[8] Many social workers spend most of their time practicing casework. Psychiatric social workers, medical social workers, school social workers, delinquency workers, and adoption workers all have regarded individual casework as their primary area of special skill. Group work, however, has also moved into all these areas as workers have acquired more knowledge about the importance of groups to individuals at every age. People in like circumstances can help each other and understand each other.

In the past ten years, family therapy has become a special kind of social work as a result of work done by such family therapy experts as Nathan Ackerman, Virginia Satir, Don Jackson, and others. These people feel very strongly that treating the individual alone will not solve the problem. Only through observing the family members as they interact with each other can the worker learn what is wrong and how to help the family change it.[9]

Caseworkers, group workers, and family workers have all learned from each other. They have also learned that they need to work with larger groups, with communities and organizations. This requires still other skills and still different knowledge as well as new applications of existing skills and knowledge. A caseworker may have several clients who have the same problem—for instance, drug abuse, with its many ramifications. Perhaps an encounter group is called for so that the clients can help each other. In addition, other persons in the community should be made aware of the extent of the problem and some of the possible alternatives available to prevent or modify it. Another example might be that of a caseworker in a welfare agency who knows that many clients are concerned about the poor service given by slum landlords. The complaint of one tenant can be brushed off, but complaints from a group may carry weight. The caseworker may thus feel that organizing a tenants' group for social action will be an important kind of help for each individual tenant. It is plain that all social workers need some skills in all three areas of social work.

Social work values

Because social work has been so concerned with values, it may be well to consider some of these values. Lists of social work values and the principles developed from them have proliferated, but the areas of agreement, not those of disagreement, stand out. Perhaps one of the best known and most widely accepted of the lists is Biestek's principles of the casework relationship between professional worker and clients, an important factor in all kinds of social work.[10] These principles, which are applicable to all kinds of relationships in the social work profession, are:

1. Individualization. Every individual, group, and community is unique and deserving of consideration as such. Each individual has dignity and worth, on his or her own merits. A person can never be viewed as one of the mob. By the same token, every social worker is an individual who knows and understands himself or herself, uses his or her own attributes and talents to the best of his or her ability —and to the clients' best good as that is determined.

The social worker's skills and knowledge are used in the context of the worker's own personality. If a beginning social worker has rather sketchy self-knowledge and understanding, at least he or she recognizes the need to improve these, and works in that direction. It is to be hoped that as other kinds of knowledge and skill are gained, the worker will improve in self-knowledge and skill because he or she will be trying to do so.

For example, a student worker was working with a mother of three young children, who was looking vainly for work. She was unskilled and had no satisfactory day-care plans for her children. The worker made various suggestions about factory work, waitress work, and sales. When she reported her efforts to the supervisor, the supervisor suggested the possibility of AFDC. The student was aghast at the thought of an able-bodied young woman "going on welfare." When she thought more about it she realized that employment was unlikely and apt to be unsatisfactory, and she concluded that her initial reaction reflected her upbringing, rather than her judgment about the propriety of welfare. In this example, the student learned something about herself, but she also learned something about the community resources and something about the needs and resources of this individual client.

2. Purposeful expression of feeling. Every individual, every group, and every community has the need to express feelings. Their right to do so is basic to social work. Emotions are as important as thoughts or beliefs or knowledge, and negative emotions are as important as positive emotions.

The leader of a group of delinquent boys noted that the group was asking fairly hostile questions of him. He accepted one member's explanation that they were tired of all these meetings, and listened to their complaints about the group's progress. Then he reviewed again the limitations placed by the court on the group, giving the boys a full explanation of the details. The group leader allowed the members to express their hostility, because they needed to vent their feelings. But he put realistic limits on the group because they needed to be reminded of them, also. His aim was support with limits.

3. Controlled emotional involvement. Every individual, every group, and every community has a right to expect that someone will be able to relate to their level of feeling. A social worker must be able to *feel* with another, not just talk with him or her. The worker need not *have* the same feelings, but he or she must show understanding of the feelings of the other person.

Mrs. Black recounted, with tears in her eyes, just how her husband had died. When she finished, she began to cry softly. Her caseworker responded by putting her hand on her shoulder without speaking. The caseworker was involved, sympathetic, responsive. She was not asked for and did not give advice. She showed nonverbally her concern.

4. Acceptance. Every individual, every group, and every community has a right to be accepted for what they are, not for what the social worker wishes they were. The social worker tries to understand where they are at this moment and to work from there. This is not the same as saying that the social worker approves of everything the client does.

Mrs. Brown has been arrested, at the instigation of a neighbor, for beating her two-year-old child. The court social worker greeted her sympathetically and asked if she would like to have someone to talk with. Mrs. Brown nodded gratefully. Without approving the client's behavior, the worker was able to indicate acceptance of Mrs. Brown as a person.

5. Nonjudgmental attitude. This precludes assigning guilt or innocence and regards blame as outside the social worker's function. The whole question of whether a person is worthy or unworthy of help seems a quaint anomaly to most social workers, though many people continue to feel that moral judgments must be made.

Carrie Smith was not an attractive client. An acknowledged prostitute, she had come to the public health clinic for counseling on family planning but suggested that she might have been exposed to syphilis. The medical social worker arranged for her to see the health officer immediately and assured Carrie that she had done the right thing to come to the clinic.

6. Self-determination. This is one of the most difficult things to give a client. Workers who are asked for help must give help and advice, but just as surely every client has a right to use or reject help, to take advice or to reject it. The client has the ownership of his problems. The concepts of individualization and acceptance include a recognition of the individual's right to self-determination.

A tenants' organization, whose efforts to see the landlord had been unsuccessful, suggested to their worker that they try picketing the landlord's home. The worker sympathized with their frustration but suggested that the landlord's neighbors might be unsympathetic and suggested an alternative action, which he would lead. The tenants were not interested and went ahead with their picketing plan.

7. Confidentiality. Finally, every client has a right to expect confidences to be kept. Every client should be able to take for granted that discussions with a social worker will not be the subject of later gossip sessions. Workers can and do discuss their clients with their supervisors—to learn how best to help—but they cannot and should not discuss their clients freely with others. In several states bills now under consideration would give social workers the same kind of immunity to legal action as that enjoyed by doctors and lawyers in protecting the confidences they receive.

All of these concepts are necessary with any size client system to form and maintain a satisfactory social work relationship. Biestek was thinking of relationships with individuals, but relationships with groups and communities require that the same principles be followed.

Important as these seven concepts and the values they represent are, however, they all produce their corollary value dilemmas. In individualizing, workers must recognize that generalization has a place in social work thinking. Human beings grow and develop at similar rates, and behavior that is acceptable at one age is neither acceptable nor normal at a later age. Also, cultural norms are different in different places and at different times. This is glaringly true in poverty and ghetto cultures, where children must learn at a very early age to protect themselves from a whole variety of dangers, to care for younger siblings, and to master a whole spectrum of important, responsible behaviors.

When does purposeful expression of feeling lose its purpose? The idea that everyone has a right to feelings and that feelings play a large part in dealing with any kind of problem must be tempered with the opposite idea that feelings in large doses can hinder both worker and client. Social workers have had to deal with their public image as bleeding hearts and do-gooders, not because of controlled emotional responses, but because of uncontrolled emotional responses. Their emphasis on human feelings has left social workers open to criticism from those who emphasize facts and figures.

The acceptance of the worker who extended sympathy to Mrs. Brown might be construed as acceptance of child beating. Clearly, acceptance and a nonjudgmental attitude are not only difficult to practice, but are also open to a great deal of question from within and without the profession. How can people have values without questioning those who have different values?

Perhaps the most difficult value to maintain and to justify is that of self-determination. Can social workers really let people decide for themselves how to bring up their children, when their ways may be harmful to those children? Can social workers really allow would-be suicides self-determination? Do people really have a right to decide whether or not they should live on public assistance or work for less than a living wage? Are social workers really in a position to protect people, to do for them, to make decisions for them? Perhaps this value, too, is open to question and qualification.

Finally, the value of confidentiality may be questioned. If welfare is right, if clients are to be encouraged to seek help with problems, why is it necessary to keep their efforts and our response to those efforts a secret? Donald Howard, in *Social Welfare: Values, Means, and Ends,* says:

> The penchant of welfare agencies to treat as confidential all transactions with beneficiaries reflects an inimical view of the need to be helped and of being helped. If this were not the case, one would expect a family service agency, for instance, not to cloak in secrecy but to divulge as a mark of honor the news that a particular family had applied to it for help or, having been helped, was now functioning happily. However, resort to family service—or any other welfare service—is seldom thought to characterize "The Family of Distinction" in the sense that

drinking a particular mineral water, smoking a certain brand of cigar, or using some other prestigious product is alleged to mark the "Man of Distinction."[11]

The preceding values are not automatically held by social workers. Most practitioners struggle throughout their lives with increasing self-awareness. This means understanding one's self and one's behavior, not only as it should be, but as it is, and trying to make the two congruent. Appendix A, The National Association of Social Workers (NASW) Code of Ethics, lists behaviors that refer directly to these values. Ethics and values are not the same, but are, like knowledge and values, directly related.

The following chapter shows something about the theory of interrelated systems and something about the interrelationships between the various methods of social work. Now we hope to show the relevance of other systems to the historical development of social work and how it has come to be a new system.

A system is a phenomenon that can be broken down into subsystems or that can combine with others to form a supersystem. Either way, the important concept is that of interrelationships, rather than of cause and effect. All parts of a system are affected by a change in one subsystem, and a change in the whole system changes all of the subsystems. Since we can never understand all of the systems that affect a given situation, we try to choose the most important interrelationships and draw conclusions from them. Inevitably, some changes can be effected consciously and rationally. Others may seem to be brought about by pure chance. But even changes that are brought about through chance affect the system and its parts.

Chapter 2 will explain systems in greater detail. The important concept is that of relationships rather than cause and effect. History shows some relationships between religion, economics, and politics as they affected the evolution of social services and their delivery.

Summary

Social welfare, social work, social intervention, and public welfare are separate entities, though connected by a common philosophy. Concern for other people has been a traditional basis for the practice of social work. Social workers need knowledge and skills, as well as values. Their knowledge must encompass the areas of human and organizational behavior, of social policy, of social research, and methods of practice. Skills in social work have included casework, which is social work with individuals; group work, which is social work with groups; and community work, which is social work with larger communities. All three skills assume an understanding of some principles of relationship. The character of the helping relationship is considered an important common factor in all types of social work.

Notes

1. Harold L. Wilensky and Charles N. Lebeaux, *Industrial Society and Social Welfare*, Publication of the Russell Sage Foundation (New York: Free Press, 1965), p. 138.

2. Wilensky and Lebeaux, *Industrial Society*.

3. Harriett Bartlett, "Social Work Practice," in *Encyclopedia of Social Work* 16 (New York: National Association of Social Workers, 1970), p. 1479.

4. Harriett Bartlett, *The Common Base of Social Work Practice* (New York: National Association of Social Workers, 1970), p. 65.

5. H. H. Goddard, *Feeblemindedness: Its Causes and Consequences* (New York: Macmillan, 1914).

6. Betty L. Baer and Ronald Fedrico, *Educating the Baccalaureate Social Worker: Report of the Undergraduate Social Work Curriculum Project* (Cambridge, Mass.: Ballinger Publishing, 1978).

7. Helen H. Perlman, *Social Casework: A Problem-Solving Process,* 12th ed. (Chicago: University of Chicago Press, 1967).

8. Florence Hollis, *Casework: A Psycho-Social Therapy,* 6th ed. (New York: Random House, 1966).

9. Virginia Satir, *Conjoint Family Therapy* (Palo Alto, Calif.: Science and Behavior Press, 1967).

10. Felix P. Biestek, *The Casework Relationship* (Chicago: Loyola University Press, 1957).

11. Donald Howard, *Social Welfare: Values, Means, and Ends* (New York: Random House, 1969), p. 193.

2

SOCIAL SYSTEMS

We hear a great deal these days about "the system," about living with it, about beating it. The term *system* means a great many things to a great many people. Natural scientists have always referred to solar systems, biologists to circulatory systems, and political scientists to capitalist or communist systems. The most recent use of the term is in computer terminology, where it is used to describe complex mechanical processes. Computers accept input of data, process it, and turn out other data or output.

The concept is useful to social workers because it provides a way of seeing relationships in time and space between ideas and things. Particularly, it is useful to see the relationships between individuals, with whom social workers are concerned, in whatever role social workers take.

What is a system?

We have two problems with the concept of systems: first, defining our own use of the word, and second, and more important, describing the existing systems that influence and are influenced by social workers. When we call something "a system" or "the system," what are we saying about it? Our label conveys our perception of a process, a variety of shifting relationships, a transformation, some influences, some results and boundaries. In our vocabulary, then, *system* means a set of dynamic general relationships that together process stimuli (inputs) through a subsystem of closer relationships, thereby producing responses (outputs). Model systems can be seen in the organic parts

16

of an individual, in an individual taken as a whole, and in groups of individuals ranging in size from pairs to billions.

For example, humans have a blood circulation system. Nerve signals resulting from emotions, fatigue, and so forth, and blood come to the heart and lungs (the subset of closer relationships), where the blood is transformed and sent on its way again until it reaches the outer boundaries of the system and returns. The system does not exist in a vacuum and may be influenced by the larger, exterior system, as when the culture provides a fatty diet, for example.

A cow may be seen as the focal point (the subset of closer relationships) of a system. She does not care what label we put on her, but we can understand something of the nature of the creature by seeing her as a process of changing food into milk and manure. If the manure fertilizes her grass, we can note the feedback in the system. If her milk nourishes the farmer who feeds her during the winter, we can see both the feedback and the influence of the larger system within which the cow lives.

Individual people can be partially described as systems. Each of us processes stimuli and comes up with responses. Each of us does this differently, since we have unique ways of perceiving and being aware of stimuli and our own capacity for response. Poets are "turned on" differently than painters and they produce different results, whose influence comes back to them in different ways.

A family, a local community, a great university, a nation, or a number of allied nations may be understood partially in these terms. The "spaceship Earth" is a system within our solar system. For all of these groups we see boundaries, a large environment that provides inputs, a focal point or points through which the exterior influences are processed and modified, some outputs, and the circular impact of the consequences as part of the next generation of influence.

In a political system we identify such stimuli as pressure group demands, underworld bribery and intimidation, political party nominations, campaign oratory and financing, and voter innocence and avarice. These are processed by government officials (lawmakers, executives, judges). The responses are visible as laws, executive orders, judicial verdicts, rewards, and burdens that in turn become grist for new efforts to influence the process. As part of the larger environment within which the political system operates, social work contributes to public policy at all three stages: input, processing, output.

Social workers identify public problems and lobby for policies to alleviate them, they sit in the councils and administration of government, and they both shape and adapt to the responses.

A social work system

Mrs. Jones came to the walk-in neighborhood center because she was unhappy with her life. Her children had been sick a great deal this winter. Her husband had recently been laid off his construction job. Several bills were past due. The landlord was threatening eviction. Mrs. Jones herself was suffering from recurring headaches. As a last straw, her mother-in-law was planning to pay a prolonged visit. A neighbor had suggested the neighborhood center, and finally Mrs. Jones decided that she had to ask for help, though she had little idea what help she could expect.

Mrs. Jones liked the warm, friendly worker immediately. Gratefully, she accepted a chair and an invitation to "tell what is bothering you." As Mrs. Jones talked, she felt as if she were being heard. She felt that her troubles were important ones. But from the worker's comments, Mrs. Jones understood that she was not the only person to have them.

When she left, she had an appointment with a doctor at the outpatient clinic and another with a family counselor. Even more important, she felt that she was doing something about her troubles. She had taken a first step.

The neighborhood center had certain functions that could be performed on the spot. Family counseling and referral to the Department of Welfare, the Department of Health, or Legal Aid, could be initiated there. To Mrs. Jones, the agency system was personalized by the worker who greeted her, asked what her problem was, and helped her answer the questions on a printed form. All the stimuli that had pushed Mrs. Jones to the agency were processed by the agency. They could not all be processed or even mentioned at once, but Mrs. Jones was able to feel that some start had been made toward alleviating some of her problems. Between her and the worker they were able to process some of the stimuli into some more satisfactory responses.

Mrs. Jones may be seen as a system; so may the worker. Both are parts of larger systems. Neither operates in a vacuum. Mrs. Jones and her family will affect the worker and the agency. The worker and the agency will affect Mrs. Jones and her family. The community in which they live affects them all. So does an even larger community. Some of the responses or output of Mrs. Jones's problems will be the result of her own efforts; some, of the efforts of other people and institutions. The responses produce feedback that will have effects on Mrs. Jones's ability to manage other problems. If her headaches are cured, she may be better able to deal with her mother-in-law. If the family has legal advice, perhaps it can deal better with the landlord. In any case, Mrs. Jones will take in new inputs or stimuli and begin with the landlord.

A process of shifting relationships between parts of a larger whole can be noted in similar examples. The process is one of changing inputs into outputs. In each case the process takes place within boundaries. It is partly autonomous and self-generating because of the feedback, and partly the pawn of exterior forces.

System terms

We have already identified some terms—*input, output, processing, feedback*. Some other terms are also used frequently:

1. *Boundaries.* The boundary of a system may be physical—as in the skin of a person—or it may be less tangible—as in an individual's attitude toward sex—depending on the variables on which we focus. The boundaries of a personal system may include all of a person's roles, or only some roles, along with that person's biological system. The boundaries of a group may be the persons in the group, or the persons and their problems, depending on which variables we choose to focus on. The boundaries of a community or nation may be physical or philosophical. A nation-state may be bordered by two oceans; a community of scholars may be bounded only by the understanding of the participants in that community.

2. *Tension, stress, strain, and conflict.* Tension means the process of being stretched. Whatever is under tension is under stress and strain. A combination of stresses and strains leads to conflict. Conflict is not necessarily good or bad, but when it occurs the system usually seeks relief. Television commercials are full of examples of individuals who are under tension, and who seek fast, fast relief. Political parties

traditionally promise to give relief from whatever problems are producing tension at a given time. Relief from tension in a family system is a reason some people seek help from social workers.

3. *Equilibrium.* A system has a tendency to achieve a balance among the various forces operating upon and within it. Equilibrium refers to a balance, either still or moving. Equilibrium, like status quo, is desirable only for the people who realize some advantage from it. A welfare department system with a balanced budget may be maintaining equilibrium at the expense of hundreds of poorly maintained recipients. From the point of view of the latter, such equilibrium is not desirable.

4. *Intersystem.* An intersystem model involves two open systems connected to each other, and therefore interacting with each other. This interaction provides an extension of the systems theory, since it can be expanded to include the entire environment or condensed to include two very small systems.

5. *Connectives.* The ties of relationship between systems are called connectives. An example might be the contract or agreement between client and worker. It might be the worker him- or herself who is a connective between client and agency. Connectives may be dysjunctive, having a negative effect on the system's present functions. Which kind of connective would a social worker aspire to be?

6. *Developmental system.* A developmental system model centers around growth and directional change. The system under consideration—individual, group, or organization—is growing, maturing, going somewhere. In this model, change is not random, or even planned, but growth-oriented. Phases and stages can be identified and predicted. This is a useful idea, but we cannot assume that future growth will reflect past growth, because there are too many other systems, too many variables to consider.

We have seen that there are several possible systems models. Each has peculiarities, but each has a common method of functioning. The components of a system that we identified follow each other in an orderly sequence: input, processing, output, feedback, and back to input.

For example, in a family, the father's new job is an input that disturbs the family equilibrium. The processing is done by the father but also by other family members who are affected by the new situation.

(A change in part of the system affects other parts of the system.) The output may be increased job satisfaction on the part of the father and adjustment to a new neighborhood by the family. The feedback may be increased general self-confidence.

This process of changing something into something else is particularly important in the field of social work because it helps to identify and explain relationships between and within individuals, small groups, and communities.

Individuals, small groups, and communities

INDIVIDUALS

Social work has traditionally been concerned with individuals' behavior and their relationships with each other and with other aspects of their environment. Social workers have long tried to learn more about why people behave as they do. Early explanations included theories of human development, ideas about cause and effect, and assumptions concerning environment versus heredity.

Human development. In this view of human behavior, individuals grow and develop at their own rate, but within broad limits. Children get teeth, and learn to walk and talk, in that order. The ages at which they do these things vary, but they must do them before they can go on to play running or singing games. A child whose development has been seriously interfered with at three months, six months, or twelve months, according to this view, will not be able to catch up. One trouble with this theory is that it assumes a more positive knowledge of human development than we have. It seems presumptuous to assume that development of white, middle-class, U.S. children is a universal norm.

Cause and effect. Some of the same objections can be made to the theory that every cause has a single identifiable effect or that every effect has a single identifiable cause. Early research in the social sciences indicated that many problems in society can be traced to many other problems. Thus poor housing predicates juvenile delinquency, as do working mothers, broken homes, and many other "causes." One trouble with this is that sorting out causes and their resulting effects is often an overwhelming task. Another trouble is that, as in the human behavior example, we simply do not know enough to be sure we know all the causes and the effects.

Environment versus heredity.   Like the two preceding approaches, the attempt to explain behavior in terms of environment versus heredity was an effort to simplify very complex social problems. At one time social scientists were willing to stake their reputations on one side or the other of this issue. The question of genetic and environmental influence could be argued, even though it was sometimes difficult to tell where one began and the other left off. A classic study of identical twins, separated at birth, served to satisfy the environmentalists, though the geneticists did not accept this proof. Terman's studies of gifted children as compared with a control group of average children indicated to the geneticists that high IQs predicted health, wealth, and happiness. The environmentalists did not agree.

To say that all of these theories were bad and have been replaced by the systems approach would be an exaggeration. But the idea of a dynamic rather than a static approach has certain advantages. So does the idea of an approach that will apply to various sizes and kinds of systems, rather than to individuals only.

A person as a system.   In the discussion at the beginning of this chapter, a system was seen to be a perception of a process, a variety of shifting relationships, a transformation, some influences, some results and boundaries. How does this apply to an individual person? Shifting relationships are evident, even before birth. The mother and child interact with each other in different ways during pregnancy, as well as during and immediately after birth. As soon as a child is born, he or she begins to be affected by other people as well as by other environmental influences. What is less evident is the baby's effect upon other people and things. A couple who have just become parents of a new baby notice tremendous changes in their lifestyle as a result of living with this tiny human being. A family that already numbers several children is also affected by an additional child. A single parent—usually the mother—must also be affected by this child. And so it goes throughout all the child's years. Not only is the child influenced by a variety of shifting relationships, but he or she in turn also effects changes on all the people and things that touch him or her. More than this, the child is affected by the genetic makeup, physical health, and all the other subsystems that make this particular individual who he or she is. Thus an individual is the result of a growing, developing process, heredity, and environment, but also his or her own unique combination of physical and mental characteristics. To try to assign a cause and effect relationship to particular characteristics would be futile. More important is the recognition that all the perceptions available at a given time may be affecting that person at that time. Seeing an individual as a system is more complex than the earlier theories, but it is also more realistic since it incorporates the infinite variety of combinations of factors available for consideration.

SMALL GROUPS

Michael Olmstead in *The Small Group* (1959) defines a small group as a plurality of individuals who are in contact with one another, who take one another into account, and who are aware of some significant commonality.[1] For our purpose we will take a small group to include from two to about twelve people.

The small group is a system that may be separate and apart from the rest of a person's life. There are therapy groups, recreation groups, groups for a variety of purposes. The group system interacts with, but has a separate identity from and in addition to the sum of the individual systems that make it.

Figure 2–1 shows a group of hospital patients interacting with each other and with the hospital administration, and indicates some of the kinds of interdependence seen in group systems.

COMMUNITY

The community can be defined as either a geographical entity or as a functional entity. We refer to a city community or to a community of interest. Like the small group, the community involves individuals who are in contact with one another, but the assumption is that in the community commonality is less significant and that the number of individuals is greater. It is possible to have a community made up of people who do not meet each other directly, as in the communities of musicians or scholars. The community is another system with which both individuals and small groups interact. The community is larger, more encompassing than the others, but this does not assume a greater or lesser degree of interaction.

FIGURE 2-1
Two diagrams of interdependence in group systems

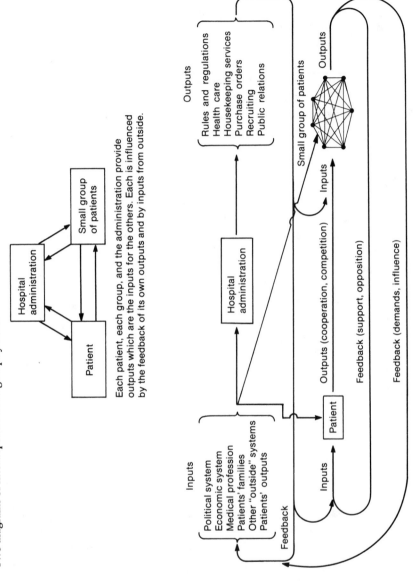

Each patient, each group, and the administration provide outputs which are the inputs for the others. Each is influenced by the feedback of its own outputs and by inputs from outside.

In the Midtown Manhattan Study of mental health, described by Leo Srole and colleagues in *Mental Health in the Metropolis,* the systems approach reflected the tremendous complexity of all the factors involved in the effort to find and explain incidences of mental illness.[2]

There are at least three types of client systems: individual, group, and community. Each of these is complex in itself and its own shifting relationships. The processes of interaction between and among the three complicate the picture still further. Yet, the understanding of some of the properties of systems theory enabled the project to proceed, rather than to bog down. The students and the field instructor learned very soon that work with individuals, families, groups, and larger communities progressed separately, jointly, or consecutively as needed. Black children being sent to a white school could be viewed as a problem rather than a solution when the client systems were understood. Input from staff, children, families, school, and community could be and was processed in a structured yet flexible way, and the output used to provide feedback—a very sensitive and sensible process. The next section attempts to describe the process by which systems can be made to change.

Social work inputs: Planned change

So far we have talked about systems interaction and interdependence, and we have talked about change in terms of growth and direction in developmental systems. With some understanding of intersystems and developmental systems, we can look at another systems model, the planned change system. In this approach, it is not assumed that change in systems need wait on spontaneous, internal change or growth. In the planned change system, the change agent (for example, the social worker) intervenes at some point in the system. The intervention seeks to proceed in a predictable, orderly way.

If we take our earlier example of Mrs. Jones, we see that of all the systems affecting her at the time she approached the neighborhood center, the two most important at that time and in that place were her family and the social agency as represented by the worker. These were not necessarily the most important systems to her once she had left the agency or before she came, but at that particular time all else assumed less importance. In the same way, a community group seeking help from an agency is acutely aware of and responsive to the agency at the point of encounter, even though prior to the encounter the agency had been quite incidental in the community experience.

The same is true of a small group that meets for the first time in a juvenile court setting. Neither the group members nor the group leader are particularly interesting to individuals until the group becomes a reality. Then the setting, the agency, and the leader assume overwhelming importance.

The steps in the planned change process used by many kinds of change agents, including social workers, follow:

1. Perception of the need for change. In Mrs. Jones's case, she became increasingly uncomfortable and unhappy with her life, but only at the suggestion of her neighbor did she decide to try to make an effort toward change. Being uncomfortable or dissatisfied or in pain may be the first step in perceiving the need for change, but the degree of discomfort that people find tolerable varies as much as do the people themselves.

2. Initiating planned change. The client may ask for help, as Mrs. Jones did. A teacher or school nurse concerned about the Jones children might have suggested strongly that she seek help. The social worker from the center, hearing of the family's problems, might have called at the home to offer the services of the center. Thus the initiator might be the client, the change agent, or a third person.

3. Establishment of a change relationship. For social workers, this has traditionally been an important part of the change process. They believe that the character or quality of a relationship is important in all kinds of human interactions, but particularly in that between clients and worker. This is true regardless of the time of interaction or of the size of the client system. A swift exchange of feeling is necessary to engender trust and engage the client system. This relationship is largely a result of input by the worker, whose attitudes, skills, and knowledge will influence what the client thinks of the worker as a person and as a professional who is ready, willing, and able to give help. When the worker or a third person approaches the client, the worker needs even more skill at relating to the client because unasked-for help is hard to accept.

4. Working toward change. Here is the heart of the process. Here is where many workers bog down. Once a need for change is felt and the relationship is developed, what happens next? The client wants to know what the worker will do. The worker wants to know what the

client will do. Some kind of mutual agreement constitutes a contract. If one step of the contract is filled, another step can follow.

5. Generalization and stabilization of change. The main test of the change agent's help is the stability and permanence of the changed behavior in the client system. Does the helping relationship promote change that continues on through the rest of the client system, or is the change localized and limited? Change for its own sake is not a desirable goal. Unless the change process can be used again and again by the client system, the change agent has not been too helpful. There are great differences in susceptibility to change among various client systems. Also, the resources and skills of the worker or the change agent help determine how well or how poorly change in one area can be continued in another.

6. Achieving a terminal relationship. Breaking off a relationship is an important part of the change process. The client system must be helped to know that its behavior has been fully successful only when it can part company from the change agent, but that this parting is desirable and necessary because it indicates that the modified client system is able to operate independently.

An enlarged and expanded explanation of the planned change process appears in Lippitt, Watson, and Wesley's *The Dynamics of Planned Change* (1958).[3] The term *change agent* is used by those authors because their references are to many professions, including social work.

Role is a concept that has become more widely used in social work in the past ten years. Role involves a set of expectations by oneself, and by others, of certain behaviors. The role of social worker involves a variety of behaviors, some involving direct service to the client, others involving indirect service. Most social workers move from role to role in the course of a single day's work. There are a number of possible ways to identify and describe social work roles. For our purpose, we will use the twelve roles outlined by McPheeters and Ryan in their monograph, *A Core of Competence for Baccalaureate Social Welfare* (1971).[4]

Roles for social workers

1. Outreach worker. A social worker who identifies and detects individuals, groups, or communities who are having difficulty (in

crises) or are in danger of becoming vulnerable (at risk) works as an outreach worker. Reaching out has a long tradition in social work.

2. Broker. The social worker who steers people toward existing services that may be of service to them is called a broker in the same way that a stockbroker steers prospective buyers toward stocks that may be useful to them.

3. Advocate. A social worker who fights for the rights and dignity of people in need of help advocates their cause. This is not one of the more popular roles at present.

4. Evaluator. A social worker who gathers information, assesses problems, and makes decisions for action is, among other things, an evaluator.

5. Mobilizer. A social worker who assembles, energizes, and organizes existing groups or new groups takes the role of mobilizer. This is most often a community organization role, though not always.

6. Teacher. A social worker whose main task is to convey and impart information and knowledge and to develop skills is a teacher. This role may or may not be played in a formal classroom situation.

7. Behavior changer. A social worker who works to bring about change in behavior patterns, habits, and perceptions of individuals or groups has the role of behavior changer.

8. Consultant. A social worker who works with other workers or other agencies to help them increase their skills and solve clients' problems is a consultant.

9. Community planner. A social worker who works with neighborhood planning groups, agencies, community agents, or governments in the development of community programs is called a community planner.

10. Data manager. A social worker who collects, classifies, and analyzes data generated within the welfare environment is a data manager. This role may be performed by a supervisor or administrator, or it may be carried out by a clerical person with the necessary skills.

11. Administrator. A social worker who manages an agency, a facility, or a small unit is operating in the role of administrator.

12. Care giver. A social worker who provides ongoing care— physical, custodial, financial—for whatever reason is acting in the role of care giver.

The important thing to remember about all the roles listed is that they are roles that combine with other roles. They are not jobs or positions. They are not necessarily related to the amount of education or training that a worker has. Most jobs in most agencies are made up of a blend of several roles. Example: A caseworker on a home visit talks with the neighbor of her client. The neighbor wants to know where she can get information on family planning. The caseworker gives the information and offers to make an appointment. Because she has had other requests, she makes a note of this, to support her feeling that the welfare department should publicize its service. Example: In a small rural agency, the supervisor allots cases, helps caseworkers with problems, supervises the clerical staff of one secretary, and prepares the office budget. Example: A caseworker visiting a new client learns of problems with the landlord. Because she recognizes the client's inability to complain, she volunteers to talk with the landlord herself. If this is not helpful, she puts the client in touch with the local rent control office.

These are examples of a caseworker who is an outreach worker, broker, data collector in the first instance; in the second, of a supervisor who is a data manager, administrator, evaluator; in the third, of a caseworker who is a broker-advocate. When we think of any job broken down into its roles, it is easier to see that the traditional skills (casework, group work, and community work) are complex and not discrete.

Summary

A *social system* is a concept that social work has borrowed from the sciences to help explain and understand the relationships between ideas and things. Concepts of human development, cause and effect, and heredity and environment were earlier efforts to see relationships.

Any system is made up of subsystems enclosed by a boundary. Input from outside is taken in, processed, and put out, causing feedback. Because we know that this process goes on, we have also accepted the idea of planned change. Change may be haphazard or it can be consciously planned, worked out, and terminated through a system's own efforts. These efforts may be supported and modified by a variety of change agents playing roles as broker, advocate, teacher, administrator, and so on.

Notes

1. Michael Olmsted, *The Small Group* (New York: Random House, 1959).

2. Leo Srole et al., *Mental Health in the Metropolis: The Midtown Manhattan Study* (New York: McGraw-Hill, 1962).

3. Ronald Lippitt, Jeanne Watson, and Bruce Wesley, *The Dynamics of Planned Change* (New York: Harcourt Brace Jovanovich, 1958).

4. Harold McPheeters and Robert Ryan, *A Core of Competence for Baccalaureate Social Welfare* (Atlanta, Ga.: Southern Regional Education Board, 1971).

3

THE HISTORY OF
SOCIAL WORK

Much of the history of social work is to be found in the history of religion, in the history of world economics and trade, and certainly in the history of political states.

The preceding chapter showed something about the theory of interrelated systems and something about the interrelationships between the various methods of social work. Now we hope to show the relevance of other systems to the historical development of social work and how it has come to be a new system.

A system, we saw, is a phenomenon that can be broken down into subsystems or can combine with others to form a supersystem. Either way, the important concept is that of interrelationships, rather than of cause and effect. All parts of a system are affected by a change in one subsystem, and a change in the whole system changes all of the subsystems. Since we can never understand all of the systems that affect a given situation, we try to choose the most important interrelationships and draw conclusions from them. Inevitably, some changes can be effected consciously and rationally. Others may seem to be brought about by pure chance. But even changes that are brought about through chance affect the system and its parts.

Some systems affecting history

Traditionally, social work history is introduced by relating the giving of alms, according to Judeo-Christian ethic. Both religions, important in Western thought, urge charity through almsgiving, that is, sharing with those less fortunate. Judaism goes back thousands of years before Christianity, which itself is now nearly 2,000 years old.

The degree to which the followers of either religion have followed its precepts is something less than complete. Some systems other than traditional religion must have an effect on social work. Economic factors must have some bearing. People who are affluent have more to share than those who have barely enough. For much of the world's history, the great majority of the people have had barely enough. Politically, the distribution of power has been linked with the distribution of wealth. Wealthy, powerful people have been in the minority but have made decisions for and about the majority. At least three systems, then, have affected the growth and development of social work: religious, economic, and political. Many other systems have also been involved; these are just the most outstanding examples of the interrelationships.

If religious influence were decisive, we might expect the rise of the Christian church to have produced a tremendous system of charity during the first thousand years after Christ. This was not the case. As Christianity became widespread, the church was intimately associated with the wealthy and powerful members of every community. Though the alms that were given were mainly the work of monks and monasteries, charity was not the all-out effort desired by the church's founder.

In England, a number of laws were passed after the waning of the Middle Ages with the purpose of discouraging an increasing incidence of vagrancy. Vagrancy and begging increased as the stability of the villages decreased and as more people were attracted to the cities. The culmination of these laws was in the legislation best known to English and U.S. social workers as 43 Elizabeth, or the 1601 Poor Law. Passed late in the reign of Elizabeth I after a long period of relative peace and security, when England was more affluent and unified than ever before in its history, it called for each locality to be responsible for its poor and old and handicapped. It was a conscious effort at change in a system that had accepted and expected beggars from time immemorial. Confiscation of church property during the reign of Elizabeth's father, Henry VIII, had deprived beggars of their usual source of maintenance. The government accepted some responsibility, and eventually, this responsibility was broadened to include employment, housing, and health. But in 1601, *local* responsibility for the poor was a new idea. Elizabeth, herself a strong monarch interested in the welfare of her people, helped in the movement toward changing attitudes toward the indigent. The beginnings of trade and industry in a country not preoccupied by threats of war helped. So did the need for beggars as potential employees. Many other systems, both developmental and planned, converged to produce the laws now generally recognized as the beginnings of responsibility for the indigent. The major provisions of the law attempted to spell out a sense of responsibility.

1. Overseers of the poor were to be appointed annually by the justices in each parish. In addition to church wardens the overseers were to include two to four "substantial householders."

2. Able-bodied persons who had no means of support were to be set to work.

3. The funds necessary for implementing the act were to be raised by taxing every householder.

4. Power was given to the justices to raise funds from other parishes in the vicinity or even within the same county if insufficient funds were available locally.

5. Overseers were authorized to bind out poor children as apprentices, subject to the consent of two justices. A "woman childe" could be bound to the age of twenty-one or marriage and a "man childe" to the age of twenty-four.

6. Local authorities, with the consent of the lords of the manors, were empowered to erect workhouses on waste lands. Building costs were to be borne by parishes or counties.

7. The mutual responsibilities of parents and children to support one another were extended to include grandparents.

8. Justices were authorized "to commit to the house of correction, or common gaol, such poor persons as shall not employ themselves to work, being appointed thereto by the overseers."[1]

These laws, crude and judgmental as they seem, were the basis for all legislation having to do with the poor in England and then in the United States for the next 300 years.

At about the same time, in 1617, St. Vincent DePaul founded the Ladies of Charity in France. His effort to foster a sense of responsibility for the poor among wealthy Frenchwomen was only partly successful, since the volunteers were not always dependable. In 1633 he founded the Sisters of Charity, who, once volunteered, were more reliable in visiting the poor, the sick, and the aged. But these were voluntary efforts in the name of religion. English poor laws saw the state as responsible for the poor.

Refinements of the Poor Law included the Settlement Act of 1662 and the Workhouse Act of 1696. The Settlement Act required the return to their own parishes of any newcomers who might be judged to become dependent on the parish to which they had moved. Not until 1795 was the act amended to require that people could be sent back to their home parish only after they had actually applied for relief. The Workhouse Act was an effort to require that paupers earn their keep through work contracted by private operators. In order to receive any relief, the laborers and their families had to live in the workhouses, separately, and under overcrowded and unsanitary conditions. Both the Settlement Act and Workhouse Act were designed to solve locally what were increasingly national and international social and economic problems. Both acts exemplified a philosophy that has continued well into the twentieth century in this country as well as in England, namely, that personal responsibility for personal problems is the accepted norm, regardless of political, economic, or social problems.

The Industrial Revolution produced much more than manufactured goods. The change from an agrarian, craft-oriented society to one in which live bodies were needed to work long hours at repetitive, boring tasks required a new philosophy. Individual people were at once more valuable in providing the new factories with workers and less valuable in that many jobs could be filled by anyone. What industrializing societies needed was a pool of available workers from which to draw. Children and women were obvious resources. So were beggars and migrants. But in order to insure the interest of these groups, the state or other political institutions needed firm rules about who might be eligible for relief, how much less than wages the relief should be, and under what circumstances relief might be given. The idea of "lesser eligibility" was very useful. It means that no one could be better off drawing relief than working. To make this a moral principle was relatively easy. It is interesting that lesser eligibility and its moral principle are still very much a part of industrialized society, even though increased automation and larger populations have continually lessened the need for unskilled workers. One concession to reality was the child labor law—both in England and in the United

States. Accounts by Charles Dickens of children working in very bad conditions help point up a major difference between nineteenth and twentieth century practice and philosophy. Nevertheless, migrant children in the United States are still exploited in practice even though the law protects them in theory. In Britain, the United States and Canada, women now work outside the home in greater numbers than ever, even though there is less need for their unskilled work. All these countries claim concern for the well-being of children whose mothers work; all these countries provide very little support for mothers to stay at home with their children.

Not until the middle of the nineteenth century were the laws reformed, and again it was at a time of relative affluence on the part of large numbers of people. It was also a time of keen interest in and concern for law and justice, as well as of vague feelings of guilt at the presence of poverty in the midst of plenty. Industrially, England was producing more wealth than ever before in its history, but many people working with factory workers, child laborers, and the unemployed knew that the good effects of production were not filtering down to all the people. Economically and religiously, the country was ready for a new reform of the poor laws. Politically, too, people with power were willing to share, if not power, at least some of the material attributes of the power. However, this same moralistic strain produced a new idea of the "worthy poor" that was built into the reforms of 1834. The gist of the idea was that there were two types of poor people: the worthy poor were deserving of help and the unworthy were not. According to Kathleen Woodroofe, in *From Charity to Social Work*:

> It was believed that the public relief of destitution, financed out of taxation as distinct from the alms of the charitable, must have a demoralizing effect on the recipient. It sapped his initiative, degraded his character, and encouraged him to be thriftless and dependent. Moreover, by raising wages above the level of mere subsistence, such relief encouraged the poor to multiply their numbers, and the wage increase was nullified.

Voluntary philanthropy, it was believed, was a far better solution to the very real problem of poverty. Helping the poor, Woodroofe asserted, was a means of "assuaging the sense of personal guilt which lay at the base of so much of the humanitarianism of the Victorian period."[2]

Meantime, in the United States, a similar movement for reform was taking place. It came as something of a surprise to the rugged individualists of the New World to find that they too had a poverty contingent. Because population was sparse and resources plentiful, the first New World communities regarded poverty as an unusual and temporary situation. Almshouses for the containment of all who could not or would not be productive were the solution in the local community. However, the English philanthropic movement found its way across the Atlantic, and a great variety of societies for the aid of certain groups were established.

As in England, the assumption that this would be a temporary situation, necessary only until the poverty group had been reclaimed and rehabilitated, gave volunteers and voluntary societies a kind of missionary zeal. But the New World had neither the experience nor the patience with nonproducers that England had. In the colonies, and later in the states, it was assumed that everyone who produced could share in the profits. This very simple economic theory was never true and never took into account the old, the young, and the handicapped. The theory also ignored the growing importance of slavery in the southern states. Though slaves were imported from Africa by all the colonies, they became an economic force in the South with the increasing importance of cotton production. Slaves were needed to plant, cultivate, and harvest cotton, but their own efforts brought them little profit except through the goodwill of their owners. As an economic institution, slavery required that owners maintain their people in reasonable health, and presumably many slave owners took care of the old and the very young, as well as of those whose productivity was essential to production. Nevertheless, slaves who produced did not share immediately in the profits but depended on the masters for their benefits. The system bred a benign dictatorship at best and exploitation at worst, and at least partly nullified psychological and religious urging toward change in a system of organized charity in the South, long after northern organizations were operating.[3] Even when some southern communities set up some organizations later in the nineteenth century, black clients were effectively excluded. The effects of slavery and all its economic, political, and psychic subsystems continued to be present in the South through the nineteenth and well into the twentieth century.

Billingsley and Giovannini, in *Children of the Storm*, say:

In one sense it might be said that until 1865 slavery was the major child welfare institution for black children in this country, since that social institution had under its mantle the largest numbers of black children. . . . Slavery affected not only black children, but also white children for the persistence of slavery as an institution even retarded reforms for white children. (In a sense slavery acted as a kind of social barometer— whatever abuses existed in the treatment of white children could be rationalized by the notion that they were treated better than black slaves.) Slavery was particularly effective in retarding improvement in the indenture system and weakening efforts at child labor reforms. . . . An unspoken value system had been established in relation to the provision of children's services: no white child shall be any worse off than any black child. No black child shall be any better off than any white child.[4]

Billingsley and Giovannini go on to describe the progress of children's services that were racist, pointing out that the orphanages of the nineteenth century excluded black children, whose only recourse was the alms house. Their main point, though, is that child welfare services have traditionally involved removing children from "unsuitable homes" rather than changing the social system to provide more suitable homes. The authors point out rightly that the Children's Aid Society excluded black children, though, "despite its exclusionary beginnings, the foster care system has been more open to black children than the institutional system of care."[5]

In the North and the West, almshouses were seen as the solution to nonproductive poverty. If people were able to produce, they could be at large; if not, they could be incarcerated. The main problem with this solution is that in spite of bad conditions in the almshouses, it was an expensive and unprofitable solution. It may have even offended the sensibilities of some of the religious members of the community. In any case, before long in the United States, as in England, voluntary societies for the relief of various categories of poor were initiated as the need was perceived by concerned people of the community.

During the mid-nineteenth century in England several scientific studies of poverty were made, notably by Charles Booth, Beatrice Potter Webb, and Edward Denison. They exposed something of the vastness of the problem of poverty in Britain. Booth's seventeen volumes of *Life and Labour of the People of London*, carefully and painstakingly researched, convinced many Victorians that voluntary aids could not reach the numbers of needy.[6] Nevertheless, the period saw the beginnings of the settlement movement. Education and encouragement in their neighborhoods, it was thought, could relieve the poor of the kinds of disadvantages most oppressive to them. One well-known settlement was started and continued by Samuel Barnett at Toynbee Hall in East London. His feeling was that the poor would benefit from the chance for "contact with those who possess the means of a higher life."[7] His colleague, Arnold Toynbee, agreed with this view and also saw that settlements were a means to social harmony, rather than political socialism. The Victorians believed in the scientific method as a means of learning about the problems of the poor. They feared the possible power of the poor, but they responded with a faith in mitigation of conflict between classes, rather than in a change in the social order. Education and understanding were to work both ways. The wealthy would learn from the poor and the poor from the rich. Settlement schools and state schools both were patterned after industrial establishments so that children would learn early the kinds of behavior that would be acceptable to adult employers. Group pressure was part of settlement house procedure, but most important was pressure from authority.

If settlement houses sound like a feeble reaction to the knowledge of poverty suddenly sprung on the Victorians, it must be remembered that the idea of any kind of social reform was new and radical in a very old country. Further, the new ideas were being put forth, not by the traditionally wealthy and powerful aristocracy, but by clergymen, professors, and business executives. Settlements were a major breakthrough. In the United States, too, the settlement movement, though later in starting, affected the lives of the poor in big cities through the efforts of people like Jane Addams at Hull House in Chicago. In the United States, the tremendous immigration of the nineteenth century forced attention on the urban poor, who were the main recipients of settlement work. Again the idea was to make the poor conform to prevailing norms, not to try to change the norms.

Nevertheless, reform was a part of the settlement movement. Education of poor people to their duties and responsibilities as citizens was stressed by Barnett and Addams. The neighborhood was seen as a subsystem of the state and the state as a subsystem of the nation. Thus, in the settlements, grass roots community work was practiced, though always within the framework of the existing organization.

The charity organization society

Amid the scarce public provisions for relief, the number and variety of voluntary organizations of the nineteenth century seemed overwhelming. An affluent class, troubled by their awareness of sin, and (according to Beatrice Potter Webb) strongly influenced by a new awareness of scientific method, seemed determined to start a new agency for each new problem as it was perceived. Charles Loch worked from 1875 until his death in 1913 to bring about some order and organization to this profligate charity. Scientific method and a strong sense of duty seemed to him to give all people a chance to achieve self-dependence. Charity could only be useful if it gave the recipient a chance at this self-dependence. To this end, he organized a group dedicated to helping those who deserved help and turning away those who did not and, further, seeing that those undeserving should not receive help elsewhere. It was not an easy task, but a Charity Organization Society (C.O.S.) report from the time indicates the system used:

Class I: Dismissed as:

Not requiring relief	1,037
Ineligible	2,273
Undeserving	1,240
Giving false address	360
Class total	4,910

Class II: Referred to:

The poor law	1,413
District agencies	1,645
Private persons	1,157
Charitable institutions	469
Class total	4,684

Class III: Assisted by:

Grants	3,293
Loans	1,039
Employment	391
Letters to hospitals	425
Labour register	623
Class total	5,780
Grand total	15,374

This table, from the C.O.S. fourth annual report (1873), shows the care, organization, and careful compilation of statistics that were the society's contribution to voluntary charity. It also shows the kinds of judgments that were made by workers about the people who applied to them. Large numbers of undeserving supplicants did not meet the society's formal requirements, which were designed to deter any who were not willing to help themselves.[8]

Even with these requirements, workers for the organization were expected to know and understand a great deal about their clientele. Thomas Chalmers, a Glasgow clergyman, emphasized the need for care in the selection and training of voluntary workers. He expected them to be of high moral ability and intelligence, and he outlined the kinds of questions they should ask and the kinds of investigations they should make. His contribution to social work was his emphasis on selection and training, as Charles Loch's was the initiation of the Charity Organization Society. Thus, we see that early social work in England was not purely casework but group work through the settlements; community organization through settlements, the Charity Organization Society; and training and education through Chalmers's guides for voluntary visitors. In this group of pioneers, Octavia Hill's emphasis on casework premises of knowledge of the individual and on the one-to-one relationship was the forerunner of the psychological emphasis in today's casework.

State and local responsibility

The nineteenth century's preoccupation with local voluntary charities cannot be said to be the result of earlier centuries' poor laws. Neither can it be said to be caused by the century's affluence, industrial expansion, scientific knowledge, or education. Rather, it was affected by all these rapidly changing systems to the end that no future period would ever again see the lack of activity in charity that prevailed in earlier times, both in England and in the United States.

In the United States, as the various states grew in power and influence, the initiation of state departments of charities and corrections or some similar organization became common. The purpose of these departments was implicitly and explicitly to save taxpayers money. Scarcity as an ideology was the accepted attitude. Whatever method of relief was given must be the least possible to maintain life. A means test and a pauper's oath were assumed to be not only desirable but necessary to make sure that no relief was given to anyone able to provide for himself. Outdoor relief, that is, relief given to people in their own homes, was considered to be more difficult to supervise and therefore more likely to corrupt.

> It is also generally known that those demanding outdoor relief are . . . members of the lowest [classes]. Regardless of all responsibility for it, they bring into the world a race of dependents, physically, morally and mentally deficient. But if, when these deficient and delinquent members of the lower classes give evidence that self-support is impossible, they are retained in institutions properly regulated, while the individuals are cared for, propagation of their kind is at least checked.[9]

Institutions such as almshouses, hospitals, and prisons were the chosen method of relief in most states. Only much later could the expense of institutional care be credited to state legislatures.

Still, U.S. citizens, like the English, felt uncomfortable with the idea of great poverty in a wealthy society. As in England, many U.S. citizens, including Charles Loring Brace, foresaw the dangers of gangs of boys adrift in large cities, preying on the unwary. Brace found his solution in organizing the Children's Aid Society of New York. The first organization of its kind, the society undertook to remove children from the unhealthy slums of New York and send them to rural homes in the Midwest where, it was hoped, they would be treated as members of the family and learn to work along with the rest of the family. If the children sometimes took on the role of indentured servants, used by families only as a source of cheap labor, this was considered as an aberration rather than a fault of the system. C. R. Henderson, in 1899, commented:

> the homeless child is taken to a childless home, or to family care where love makes room for one more object of mercy and hope. . . . The old sad history is forgotten; with a new home begins new memories and a new career.[10]

Other kinds of voluntary organizations operated much as in England in response to perceived need. And, as in England, the Charity Organization Society, first in Buffalo, tried to bring order from chaos through the same principles of investigation, registration, cooperation, and friendly visiting as laid down by the London society.

Gradually, through the end of the nineteenth century and into the twentieth, the charity-giver and the radical joined forces, according to Jane Addams. From a firm conviction that poverty caused the delinquency of the individual came some recognition that the capitalistic system in a democratic framework produced more equality for the rich than for the poor. By the outbreak of World War I, social workers and reformers had joined forces, at least in some matters, and social work had left the era of friendly visiting to become more professional and less apologetic about its function. Some people like Mary Richmond were beginning to press for training and education and even salaries for social workers.

Mary Richmond

Mary Richmond happened into social work when she accepted the job of assistant treasurer to the Charity Organization Society of Baltimore at $50 a month. As she learned about the organization, she posited that charity is a great social force that should and could cooperate with workers of every variety of social belief. Her philosophy combined with an ability to administer and a genius for organization, and from assistant treasurer in Baltimore she moved to the position of general secretary of the Philadelphia Society for Organizing Charity. Her favorite message was that of the necessity to combine casework with social reform.

When she became director of the Charity Organization Department of the Russell Sage Foundation in New York, she became involved in training and educating social workers, and it was then that she started work on her famous conceptualization of the social work process. She called it *Social Diagnosis* when it was published in 1917, and it is a classic today.[11] For the first time, the social work process was described systematically in terms of fact-finding, diagnosis, planning, and treatment. Though the emphasis is on the worker's activity, participation by the client is implicit. Her concern was with social casework and with a generic process by which all workers could proceed. Workers had been doing most of the kinds of tasks outlined by her for many years, but her clear, concise writing helped to pull the process together.

The work of Mary Richmond was another of the important influences on the development of the system of social work. Her writings came at a time when the current system was beginning to lose momentum. Richmond's emphasis on method did not ignore the need for values, sensitivity, and a helpful relationship; but because the method was a specific new tool it was possible for workers to follow procedure implicitly, with little regard for the client's feelings. Richmond's intent had fewer followers than her method.

Freud and psychiatry

The effect of the writings of Sigmund Freud on the practice of social work, first in the United States and later in England, can hardly be overestimated. It seemed as if the system were looking for a change, a new direction, and the field of mental health provided the input. Custodial care for the mentally afflicted had been the rule until the late nineteenth century when Freud's work began to be published. Though Freud claimed success only for his work with neurotic patients, his theories of the dynamics of personality and of the unconscious focused interest on the causes of mental illness and the possibilities of treatment, rather than on custodial care. Clifford Beers's account of his institutional experience, A Mind That Found Itself, gave impetus to this interest.[12] A committee organized for mental hygiene reported to the National Conference on Charities and Corrections in 1917 that the one science that had most to contribute, then or ultimately, to social work was unquestionably the science of the mind.[13]

The entry of the United States into World War I brought new problems and new clients to social workers, especially to those in the private sector. They were, for the first time, dealing with people whose problems were not necessarily financial. Newly discovered psychoanalytic theories helped to explain and treat problems that seemed to originate in the individual's psyche. Caseworkers spoke of personal adjustment as the major purpose of their work, rather then personal independence.

Freud was not the only source of the new theories. Jung, Adler, and Rank all contributed to the new emphasis on psychic problems and their solutions.

Differences between England and the United States

Important as theories were, they appealed more to U.S. and Canadian than to English caseworkers. Different systems in each country produced different inputs, processing, and output. The United States's traditional emphasis on individual difference and "rugged individualism," bolstered by the Puritan ethic and an era of economic affluence, all combined to distract social workers from social reform while they concentrated on individual adjustment. In England, social reform had gotten off to a better start. English social workers were more concerned with individualizing *services* to meet the needs of laborers, children, and women, than with the personalities of the people. The idea of the welfare state was not anathema but a reasonable goal to achieve the best life for the greatest number.

The United States had made some effort to organize voluntary contributions to voluntary agencies during and after World War I (this kind of activity appealed to the business community as a means of making social work more efficient), but not until well after the beginning of the Great Depression in 1929 was any formal national effort mounted toward public welfare. The Depression, with its accompanying unemployment and loss of private savings, provided a stimulus that local and federal governments could not ignore. At the beginning, the ideas of individual effort and expected recovery were employed by the federal administration under Herbert Hoover. Private welfare agencies were receiving less money and trying to do more work. State and local authorities were finding that their funds were grossly inadequate to deal with the number of applicants. Social workers found that personality analysis did not solve the problems of the jobless or the homeless. No one was feeling affluent. The Puritan ethic seemed to have gone astray, and powerful business interests were not powerful enough to reelect a Republican administration. Roosevelt's New Deal was the first dramatic entry of U.S. government into the field of public welfare.

> The only thing we have to fear is fear itself. Our distress comes from no failure of substance. We are stricken by no plague of locusts. . . . Our greatest primary task is to put people to work. . . . I am prepared under my constitutional duty to recommend the measures that a stricken Nation in the midst of a stricken world may require.[14]

The first federal program to provide some relief for states' welfare efforts was the Federal Emergency Relief Administration (FERA), which at first provided some $500 million. Half of this amount was provided to states on a matching basis, half to states whose unemployment was so great or whose resources were so depleted that no matching funds were available. All FERA funds were to be administered through public agencies and by professional social workers. While this program provided the first venture of the federal government into public welfare, its main objective was to provide unemployment relief for those persons who had lost their jobs as a result of the Depression. Unemployables, such as old people, children, and the handicapped, were not eligible. Work was considered a better solution than direct relief, and many public works projects resulted. The term *emergency* indicated that the program was expected to be of short duration; and it was, partly because of criticism from various quarters. It was followed by the Works Progress Administration, the National Youth Administration, and the Farm Security Administration. All of these provided more experience with federal-state-local cooperation, but none of them provided the kind of permanent organization for public welfare that was clearly needed. To this end, Roosevelt appointed a Committee on Economic Security made up of the secretaries of labor, treasury, and agriculture, and the attorney general and the Federal Emergency Relief administrator. In January 1935 the Economic Security Bill was submitted and, after many amendments, passed by the Congress.

The social security provisions finally became law on August 14, 1935, and because they had been watered down and categorized they fell far short of a welfare state. We can only surmise whether or not less attention to psychiatry and more to social reform might have produced earlier work on a better social security proposal, but the 1935 law hardly lived up to its title. It provided two proposals for social insurance, three proposals for general assistance, provisions for maternal and child welfare services, aid to the blind and to dependent and crippled children, and a plan to strengthen public health work. It provided nothing for the unemployed able-bodied worker whose plight had been the reason for government involvement in welfare. Its old-age pension proposal included a means test, and its social insurance provisions insured little. Nevertheless, the federal government was finally in the business of social welfare, and from 1935 to the entry of the United States into World War II in 1941, the country and the social work profession tried to sort out the workable aspects of the law.

In England, while the Depression also struck a bitter blow, some aspects of social welfare had already been taken over by the state. Workman's compensation, old-age pensions, and compulsory contributory sickness and unemployment insurance had been in effect since before World War I. These and other public assistance programs had been occupying the English social worker's time and energy during the psychiatric era in the United States. England's postwar period was less prosperous than that of the United States, and its faith in the Puritan ethic had not persisted into the twentieth century. England was generally better prepared to deal with economic disaster in the thirties and to move into a true welfare state after World War II.

With its usual traditional reluctance to move into foreign entanglements, the United States became involved in World War II only after her allies had spent two years fighting. Fascism had been viewed with less alarm than communism. The United States had domestic problems that were overwhelming, and there was a general desire for peace and isolation. Nevertheless, the government's involvement in public welfare had paved the way for compliance with Allied aims even before the Japanese bombing of Pearl Harbor. Again, the social workers of the nation found themselves with clients whose needs were other than financial problems. The American Red Cross, the United Service Organizations, and other voluntary agencies geared up again, and family service agencies pursued their Freudian way. Nevertheless, the Depression, followed by World War II, suggested to some social workers that national, even international, planning might be the reasonable task of social work. Surely even the best-adjusted individual could not be expected to deal with such major catastrophes.

After World War II, social work in the United States played a larger part in all sorts of community organization, community development, and community planning. Hesitantly at first, then with more assurance, the profession began to add to the theories and tasks that seemed to come within the purview of social work. At the same time, professional education became a more and more important preoccupation with social workers who had been practicing for most of their lives. The profession began to differentiate among its three main methods—casework, group work, and community organization. The Council on Social Work Education attacked the task of identifying and describing the kinds of studies needed by all social workers for the practice of all kinds of social work. According to Werner Boehm in his article on social work education in the *Encyclopedia of Social Work*, in recent years schools of social work have usually accepted one of three forms for teaching social work methods.

1. The first model consists of schools making available a concentration in a combination of methods, frequently casework and group work on the premise that there is similarity if not identity of principles between these two methods.

2. Other schools have made it possible for students to acquire a generic base for the methods on the premise that there are some principles and concepts in each method that are not method-specific but social work-specific and therefore need to be possessed by all social workers who, in addition to their generalist function, also need a specific method-determined function.

3. Still a third model operates on the premise that society currently needs a social worker with skills in several methods of intervention. Some schools thus seek to train a "generic" social worker whose knowledge and skill are undifferentiated as to method. These schools, in fact or in theory, question the validity of the concept of method differentiation.[15]

So important was social work education seen to be that, during the fifties and sixties, many agencies, both public and private, were willing to finance graduate studies for workers who were already practicing. Education generally, and social work education in particular, received tremendous support during those difficult decades—again influenced by an era of economic affluence, the broadening power base in politics, and a general faith in education to overcome the evils of urbanization, industrialization, prejudice, and bigotry. Social workers were in the vanguard. Group workers, like caseworkers, were carving out new empires, trying new methods, and researching new theories.

At the same time, during the 1960s, the nation, first under Kennedy and then under Johnson, became involved in an effort to put an end to poverty. Dramatic in its conception, the program followed a number of earlier pilot programs aimed at improving the quality of life for persons at the very bottom of the economic ladder. For the first

time poverty was to be attacked at its roots. The program was to involve a new federal organization, was to work directly with communities rather than through the states, and was pledged to involve
maximum feasible participation. The last requirement proved to be a
bone of contention, but also to be one of the lasting effects of the program. Most of the projects, including Community Action Programs,
Head Start, Legal Aid, and Vista, involved poor people. The plan was
that the poor should be actively involved in planning and staffing.
For various reasons, the federal administration preferred not to use
existing welfare departments and regarded professional social workers as supporters of the establishment. While social workers resented
this attitude, it forced them to reconsider their roles in working with
the poor and spurred more interest in the area of community work
and efforts at changing the larger systems. Client participation in
planning and programming was sometimes successful and sometimes not, but social workers learned that they could and should become involved with different systems in different ways.

With the seventies came economic recession and conservative, authoritarian federal administration. Beulah Compton, in *Social Welfare
and Social Work*, sums up:

> The late 1960s and the 1970s were years of confusion—years when
> many of those who worked in social welfare felt that they had no
> friends. They were attacked on one side by the far Left and on the other
> by the far Right, and their clients were critical as well. It was a time
> when newly formed evaluative methods were used with great aban-
> don. It was assumed, contrary to good research principles, that if some-
> thing could not be proved to be of significant help, it was a failure . . .
> the result of all this was that programs for the poor were curtailed. Not
> only were such programs curtailed, but the general feeling arose that
> the poor had had an opportunity through the Great Society and that it
> had been proved that they could not be helped.[16]

Both Presidents Nixon and Carter were impressed with the need
for accountability to the taxpayer rather than to the client. Nixon's
revenue sharing plan proposed greater responsibility on the part of
state and local government, and less federal administration. The Carter reforms emphasized the dichotomy of working and nonworking
poor, and proposed subsidized jobs and job-training programs to be
administered with federal guidelines.

The first term of the Reagan administration promoted budget and tax cuts. The second term dealt with the ever-mounting deficit by still greater cuts in human services. It seems certain that more programs will be cut down or cut out. The phrase *truly needy*, reminiscent of *worthy poor*, has become a respectable and respected watchword. Despite the many social problems and search for their solution, both in the United States and in the United Kingdom, there seems a preference for residual rather than institutional approaches to welfare.

As we saw at the beginning of this chapter, the interdependence of many systems have affected the process of welfare development. Economics and politics seem at the present time to play more important roles than religion. Inflation and unemployment vie for first place in problem priority in the view of Americans and British. Until these are overcome or replaced by some more pressing problems, welfare reform is likely to be ignored or at least overlooked.

Summary

The history of social work has been closely tied to the history of religion, of economics, and of politics. Social responsibility has its roots in a pre-Christian era and has taken different forms at different times in history. Residual and institutional views of social problems have contributed to theories of social welfare and social work. The English poor laws and settlement laws provided models for public responsibility in the new world, and some of the basic premises of individual versus public guilt still have an effect today. The Victorians' respect for scientific method led to efforts at organizing and quantifying charity. Freud's studies of personality development led the way to individualizing social work. With the entrance of national governments into the welfare field, social work and social work education have become full-fledged professional fields both in the United States and in England.

Notes

1. Helen M. Crampton and Kenneth K. Kaiser, *Social Welfare: Institution and Process* (New York: Random House, 1970), p. 7.

2. Kathleen Woodroofe, *From Charity to Social Work* (Boston: Routledge & Kegan Paul, 1962), p. 17.

3.   Robert Fogel and Stanley Engerman, *Time on the Cross*, 2 vols. (Boston: Little, Brown, 1974).

4.   Andrew Billingsley and Jeanne Giovannini, *Children of the Storm* (New York: Harcourt Brace Jovanovich, 1972), p. 24.

5.   Billingsley and Giovannini, *Children of the Storm*, p. 35.

6.   Charles Booth, *Life and Labour of the People of London*, 17 vols. (London: Macmillan, 1902).

7.   Henrietta Barnett, *Canon Barnett, His Life, Work and Friends*, vol. 1 (London: John Murray, 1919), p. 307.

8.   Charity Organization Society, *Fourth Annual Report, 1873*, p. 2.

9.   Proceedings of the Sixth Annual Conference of Charities, *The Prevention of Pauperism* (Chicago, 1879), p. 214.

10.   Proceedings of the 26th National Conference of Charities and Corrections (Cincinnati, 1899), pp. 12–13.

11.   Mary Richmond, *Social Diagnosis* (New York: Russell Sage, 1917).

12.   Clifford Beers, *A Mind that Found Itself* (Garden City: Doubleday, 1935).

13.   Owen Copp, "Bearing of Psychology on Social Casework," in Report for Committee Organized for Mental Hygiene, *Proceedings of the National Council of Social Work* 44 (Pittsburgh, 1917), pp. 104–12.

14.   Franklin Delano Roosevelt, First Inaugural Address, March 4, 1933, in *Public Papers and Addresses*, vol. 2, pp. 11, 13, 15.

15.   Werner Boehm, "Education for Social Work," in *Encyclopedia of Social Work*, vol. 1 (New York: National Association of Social Workers, 1971), p. 260.

16.   Beulah Compton, *Introduction to Social Welfare and Social Work* (Chicago: Dorsey Press, 1980), p. 514.

PART TWO

Direct service delivery

Most social workers throughout history have been involved in providing services directly to clients. They have offered and still do offer goods and services to individuals, families, and groups. Their relationships have been close and intimate. To most people, including most social workers, this is the very heart of social work. Still, almost from the beginning, the usual method of delivering services and goods has been through an agency, either voluntary or state-funded. As we saw in Chapter "3," history has vacillated between private and public funding for social services. The church, through monasteries, and the state, through the poor laws, almshouses, and outdoor relief set the pattern. Charity organization societies, settlements, state pension funds, and the Social Security Act all involved planning, administration, and execution by some private or public agency. By 1980 we see a vast bureaucratic network, systematically related, that provides nearly all social services. The exception is a relatively small group of private practitioners who provide social services for fees. Even these are likely to receive some of the funding through governmental purchase of service. Part Two of this book will deal with direct services. It will take up services to individuals, families, and small groups. Social workers need certain knowledge, skills, and values to deal with these various-sized client systems. In many ways these are the same, and in other ways the knowledge, skills and values are different. Traditionally and historically these direct service methods have developed separately: casework first, then group work, and last, work with families. Even now, some social workers argue that families have always been a part of casework, but the literature indicates that family work may be the fastest growing method, about to catch up with the older categories.

4

SOCIAL CASEWORK

Social work is a process of intervention between two or more systems by one or more change agents. The process of intervening on an individual basis has been known, traditionally, as casework. Helen Harris Perlman says, in the first chapter of her book, *Social Casework: A Problem Solving Process*: "To attempt to define social casework takes courage or foolhardiness or perhaps a bit of both."[1]

However, Perlman, who is an authority in the field, goes on to suggest the following definition:

> Social Casework is a process used by certain human welfare agencies to help individuals to cope more effectively with their problems in social functioning. . . .
>
> The nucleus of the casework event is this: a person with a problem comes to a place where a professional representative helps him by a given process.[2]

Florence Hollis, another leading authority, says:

> Central to casework is the notion of "the person in his situation" as a three-fold configuration consisting of the person, the situation and the interaction between them.[3]

While experts in the field respect Perlman and Hollis as two different kinds of practitioners with differing outlooks, others can see remarkable agreement in their versions of the casework process. (Additionally, perhaps, we can appreciate the similarity between these two versions and the definitions of social work in Chapter 1.)

These definitions indicate an awareness of the importance of the individual as part of various systems, outside him- or herself. Perlman emphasizes the importance of *the agency* with all its subsystems

and supersystems. Hollis indicates that the *situation* with all its ramifications is the concept to be dealt with.

Both agency and situation are important systems, not only in intervening with individuals, but with families, groups, and communities as well. There are some differences between casework, family
therapy, group work, and community work, but there are also similarities. With all sizes of client systems, the planned change process is
followed.

Initiating the planned change process

A variety of situations and initiatives may lead to social work intervention. The individual or group directly involved, the family, public
officials, social work agencies, or others concerned may initiate intervention.

In the case of an individual, the perception of need for change may
be a real discomfort, pain, or deprivation. A woman whose husband
has abandoned her with no means of support for her small children
does not have to wonder whether or not she really needs change. On
the other hand, alcoholics or drug addicts may not feel any need to
change their lives, though the need may be quite obvious to other
people. Dissatisfaction with one's marriage, one's job, or one's housing may be enough to send some people looking for help, while others will not even think of doing so.

Another important consideration following the first step of perceiving a need for change is the individual's ability to ask for help.
Even a strongly felt need may not lead to intervention if the person is
inhibited about seeking assistance. Asking for help is a very difficult
thing for many people. Most of us do not like to feel dependent on
others for coping with problems that we think other people in our circumstances solve by themselves. Students frequently experience difficulty asking help from teachers; children dislike asking their parents
for emotional help; old people dislike asking help from younger ones
when it involves loss of independence and an admission of decreased
competence.

Still, many requests for change come from the person most concerned, and some social workers have felt that this ability to ask for
help is necessary before service can be rendered effectively.

The second possibility is that the felt need for change is transformed into action only through the action of some other party. Teachers, physicians, and judges are among the professional people who promote change initiation on behalf of others. Parents frequently initiate intervention on behalf of their children or other people's children. Friends, neighbors, and relatives may be the instigators of change on behalf of anyone they know.

The third possibility is that the initiator of change may be the change agent himself. More and more, it seems evident that the people most in need of help may have no intention of asking it, or may have no friends or relatives to instigate help. For these people the outreach of social work is vital. Social agency branches are sometimes located in residential neighborhoods. Advertisements are placed in public transport or on television publicizing such services as abortion referrals and crisis counseling along with a telephone number. In one mental health center, social workers went out knocking on doors and introducing themselves in supermarkets, much as political candidates do, to make themselves known in the neighborhood. In such cases the social workers make the first contact and their potential clients respond rather than initiate the process of change. However the change is initiated, much of the rest of the process depends on the feelings engendered in the beginning and during the next step of establishing the change relationship.

The change relationship, as Biestek suggests, is essential to the casework process.[4] Indeed, it is essential to the entire social work process. While the establishment of the relationship seems a tremendous responsibility for the worker—and certainly it is—still there can be no professional progress without it. The worker is able to give it his or her attention, while the client, who is confused and upset by his or her need, may have little idea what to expect from the worker.

If the worker can put him- or herself in the client's place, even briefly, and try to imagine the appearance of the office, the receptionist, and especially the all-important worker, he or she may be able to get some idea of the client's feelings. Some students have gone to a clinic or a welfare agency to apply for assistance in order to glimpse what it might feel like to be on the other side of the desk. Perlman says, "The person who comes as a client to a social agency is always under a stress."[5] Particularly stressful is the situation that is interracial or intercultural. Because most agencies employ predominantly white, English-speaking workers, a client from a minority group may expect and unfortunately may encounter a worker who does not understand him or his problem, or who appears to lack this important understanding. Nevertheless, the worker who makes the effort, who feels sympathetic, who tries to put him- or herself in the client's place has a good chance of relating to the client. It could be hoped that as workers recognize their own limitations and blind spots, they will work toward erasing them.

Important as the worker's feeling and involvement are, they cannot take the place of knowledge and skill. The worker knows information and resources that the client does not, and the worker has skills in bringing the client together with this knowledge. To be most helpful to the client, the worker must not be carried away by sympathy, but must be able to stand off and look at the client and the client's problem dispassionately, to find a balance between involvement and distance.

The interview

As a result of some initiative, either by a prospective client or another concerned person, a contact between the change agent and the individual is established. The initial contact takes the form of an interview where the feeling of empathy we have been considering seems most important, even before the interview begins. Alfred Kadushin, in his book *The Social Work Interview*, says "social workers spend more time interviewing than in any other single activity. It is the most important, most frequently employed skill."[6] Even given Kadushin's bias, there is no doubt that interviewing is important, and it is a learned skill. Very few workers know instinctively how to interview.

The word *interview* may be slightly overwhelming to a new worker who does not know how to proceed, but because he or she is trying to feel with the client, he or she makes an effort to be warm, interested, and at ease. And that is the first step in the interview. Since this is the first step in many social relationships, what is different about conducting an interview? First of all, both client and worker know that they have met because the client has a problem he or she hopes the worker can help with. If the client does not understand this—if he or she is, for example, elderly, confused, or ill—then the worker's first efforts should be directed toward helping the client to understand what he or she is there for. If the client knows the purpose of the visit, he or she should be encouraged to tell his or her story in his or her own words, as easily as possible. Sometimes clients do not verbalize easily. They may need a great deal of help and must be asked many leading questions. On the other hand, some workers are more at ease asking questions and filling in forms than in listening to the client tell the story in his or her own way. Such a worker may interfere with the client's chance to explain his or her own position. Sometimes, the agency requires a certain amount of information, which the worker must get. In any case, a balance between initiative and restraint is important, and the worker's warmth and interest are vital so that the client will feel accepted as a part of the new system. Besides the client's verbal communication, the worker must be keenly aware of the nonverbal cues, such as nervous movements, trembling hands, blushing or pallor, shortness of breath, or a variety of other signs that are seen rather than heard. The worker should also be keenly aware of his or her own emotional signals. Does he or she find himself feeling particularly good about this client?

For example: When Ms. Adams came into the worker's rather small office, she was flushed, somewhat disheveled, and bright-eyed. As the worker shook hands with her, she thought she detected the odor of alcohol on Ms. Adams' breath. Ms. Adams, the mother of three small children, wished to know if she were eligible for AFDC (Aid to Families with Dependent Children). As she described the difficulty she had had in making the effort to come to the agency, the worker decided that she was under considerable nervous strain, but that she was certainly not drunk.

Ms. Adams said, in a rush, that her husband had left home a week before after a quarrel over money. She had thought the quarrel not particularly different from many others and had not even felt upset when Mr. Adams did not come home that evening. She had money, and she felt sure he would return when "he got over being mad." Now he had been gone for a week, and her money was gone. She confided in her friend and neighbor, who was sympathetic but who advised her to seek help. Ms. Adams had no idea where to turn for help. Her family and her husband's family lived 2,000 miles away. Desperately, she searched the yellow pages of the telephone book and called a number for Family Service. She had been advised to come in this morning, but she had had to bring her children and she was concerned about their behavior in the waiting room. The worker responded to this immediate concern by asking if Ms. Adams would like to have them with her during the interview. Ms. Adams said she certainly would. When she returned with three little boys, aged three, four, and five, the worker produced a pack of cards and asked the boys if they would like to build a card house. Ms. Adams actually smiled and was clearly relieved.

This brief account covers the first three stages of planned change. Which statements refer to the perception of need for change, which to the initiation stage, and which to the beginning of the relationship? Why were the children brought in?

Contract

If all goes well, before the first interview is over, both client and worker know what the problem is and what alternative actions may be taken to alleviate it. This recognition of what each is expected to do, and what each can expect of the other, is known as a *contract*. This is a rather impressive-sounding word for what may be a very informal agreement. Sometimes, a contract may be only setting the time and place for another meeting. Sometimes, both worker and client agree on certain action that will be taken before their next meeting. In any case, the basis for the contract is that it involves mutual expectations. Both worker and client are responsible for doing something. Together, worker and client have *assessed* the situation at least tentatively. They have made a tentative *plan* and set tentative *goals*. These are important components of social work intervention. The clear recognition by each of the tasks for client and worker is known as a contract.

William Schwartz, whose writing deals mainly with groups but whose concept of contract is applicable to all of social work, lists five central social work tasks:

1.   The task of searching out the common ground between the client's perception of his own need and the aspects of social demand with which he is faced. [The worker tries to find out exactly what the client sees as his problem, and whether this seems to fit with what

seems to be the reality of his situation. "Common ground" is a reconciliation between what is and what the client would like.]

2. The task of detecting and challenging the obstacles which obscure the common ground and frustrate the efforts of people to identify their own self-interest with that of their "significant others." [Obstacles may be real or imagined, but the worker's task is to decide which is which. Once identified, the obstacles may be challenged or dealt with by worker and client together, so that the client will not see himself as alienated from other people who are important to him, that is, his "significant others."]

3. The task of contributing data—ideas, facts, and value concepts —which are not available to the client and which may prove useful to him in attempting to cope with that part of social reality which is involved in the problems on which he is working. [The worker probably knows about community resources, which he can suggest. His own agency may offer some services that the client can use. More than that, the worker's knowledge of human behavior, social policy, or his own human values may be new to the client.]

4. The task of "lending a vision" to the client, in which the worker both reveals himself as one whose own hopes and aspirations are strongly invested in the interaction between people and society and projects a deep feeling for that which represents individual well-being and the social good. [The worker is not currently under stress, and he has a background of success in dealing with people and their problems. He can share his experience and his values with the client, putting himself into the relationship, showing his concern and hope for a successful resolution.]

5. The task of defining the requirements and the limits of the situation in which the client-worker system is set. These rules and boundaries establish the context for the "working contract" which binds the client and the agency to each other and which both client and worker assume as their respective functions. [Having shown the client that the worker is interested, that the agency offers services, and having offered some hope for resolution of the problem, the worker sets the stage and provides the rules that both the client and worker will follow. It is important to note that the emergence of a contract is part of the change process, but that the development of a relationship precedes any effort to establish the contract.][7]

The caseworker, striving to put these central tasks into practice, will listen carefully and sympathetically to the client's version of the problem as he or she sees it. The worker will then try to describe what the agency can or cannot do and, more specifically, what he or she personally can and cannot do. The client should have an opportunity to accept or discard these proposals. If client and agency perceive some common ground between client need and agency services, then they have a contract.

For example: Knowing that her children were taken care of, Ms. Adams proceeded to relate a story of marital, employment, housing, and money problems. She had no idea where her husband had gone and no idea what she could do until he returned. She hoped the worker could help. The worker outlined the agency purposes and policies, the arrangement for temporary aid, and the necessity for making an effort to find Mr. Adams. At first, Ms. Adams protested that she did not want to find him. If he did not care about her and the children, she did not want him to return. But how, the worker asked, could she support herself and her children? Ms. Adams did not know, but she felt sure that her husband would return, would be sorry for what he had done, and everything would be all right. The worker said she hoped that this would be the case but explained again that in the meantime, some effort would have to be made to find Mr. Adams. Ms. Adams asked angrily if the worker would like to have *her* husband checked on by the police. The worker replied that she knew it was hard to consider this possibility but that this was one of the requirements for getting aid from this agency.

Which of Schwartz's central tasks are exemplified in the foregoing? Did the worker respond appropriately to Ms. Adams' anger? Should the worker have explained the reasons for the search policy? How else could Ms. Adams' objections have been handled?

Lawrence Shulman, in describing the contract, says:

> This contract will serve as a guide for the work they will do together. It has been openly arrived at and may be openly changed. While it stands, however, it serves to clarify the nature of the group's work and protect this work from "subversion" by group members, the worker or the agency.[8]

If we substitute the word *client* for *group* and *group members*, we have a good picture of what goes in this step of the casework process.

The work referred to by Shulman is the real heart of the casework process. Here alternative plans are developed, considered, discarded, or accepted. Important in this stage is the worker's recognition of the client as an individual with a right to work out his or her own destiny, to manage his or her own life. Because a client has decided, or been forced, to ask for help does not mean that he or she is unable or unwilling to participate in his or her own plan. It is tempting to tell people what to do when they ask for advice, particularly when the solution seems obvious. But advice is rarely taken, and if it is taken, the outcome is rarely successful. Clients are more likely to make a success of their own plans than of an expert's. Social workers have worked hard and long—and continue to do so—to get rid of their images as givers of advice, and people who tell others what to do.

In making a contract, the worker and client are really working together in an interdependent and symbiotic way. Each needs the other to carry out part of the contract. On mutual understanding and respect will depend the next stage of the planned change process. Generalization and stabilization of change is the main test of the change agent's or worker's help. If the work jointly decided on is tried out in a specific situation and can be carried out in other situations and in other settings, the change can be said to be generalized and stabilized. If, on the other hand, the client is trying to please the worker, or to do what the worker wants him or her to do, then the change is probably not stabilized or generalized. The worker who tries to do everything *for* the client instead of *with* the client, has made impossible the generalization of change, because the client will be unable to do what the worker has done. Questions to be asked about the generalization and stabilization of change are: Can the client feel a sense of satisfaction and achievement as a result of the efforts, and point to feelings before and after with pleasure?

For example: Ms. Adams said she certainly had to have money—and soon. How soon could she get some? The worker suggested that together they look at the most pressing needs and try to figure out an emergency budget. Ms. Adams said she must have bread and milk and eggs for the boys. The worker agreed that these were necessities and congratulated Ms. Adams on seeing the important things first. Ms. Adams knew nothing about her husband's finances and had no idea if he had a checking account. In any case, she had never written a check. She reminisced about her life before she was married. She had worked in a mail-order house, received an envelope containing cash each week, and had no one to report to as to how she spent the money. The worker said that must seem very good to her now. But in the meantime, how far would $20 go toward groceries for a week? Ms. Adams knew exactly what she paid for various items and agreed that that sum would certainly help. The worker asked her to bring receipts and the boys' birth certificates next week. By that time, the application would be underway. When Ms. Adams told the boys to pick up the cards, they did so with only a little complaint. The worker told them that they had been very nice guests and invited them back next week. Ms. Adams smiled and thanked the worker. She said she did not like the idea of searching for her husband but she guessed it was necessary. The worker gave her an appointment card for the same time next week.

What was the work being done in this exchange? How was interdependence shown? Should the worker have let Ms. Adams talk more about her early life? If so, why? What systems other than the family are referred to in this passage? How do they affect Ms. Adams? Even in this first interview, can you see instances of contract and stabilization of behavior?

Finally, the last step of the change process must come. With some resolution of the problem, some achievement of a goal, the relationship must terminate. To the surprise of many clients and many workers, this is often a painful step. If it was difficult to begin a relationship, it is also difficult to end one. Again, the worker may have strong feelings about himself or herself and the client, but must remember that the client has a bigger stake, has taken more risks, and feels more dependence. Therefore, it behooves the worker to help the client to terminate, despite the worker's own feelings. The worker must recognize and accept feelings of separation, at the same time recognizing the client's difficulty in accepting the end. The client may be resentful, hostile, or deliberately uncaring. Like any separation, this one will cause fears and doubts, and perhaps regression to earlier behavior. Because the worker has tried to develop the relationship, he or she may feel guilty about breaking it off. The client may well perceive this guilt and try to make the most of it. If anything, the worker is expected to be more accepting and understanding in this stage than in any preceding stage. The worker must also be firm about setting limits.

For example: Ms. Adams returned for her appointment the next week without the children. She would not need any more assistance. Mr. Adams had returned on Sunday, and she would have no more financial problems. The worker said she was very glad to hear that. Would Ms. Adams be interested in marital counseling? Ms. Adams said, in an annoyed tone, that this would not be necessary. She was certainly glad that she had not let the agency search for her husband. The worker said that she was glad it had not been necessary but reminded Ms. Adams that the agency was available if the need should arise.

If you were the worker, would you have offered counseling? If so, why? Why do you think Ms. Adams refused the offer? What feelings are shown by Ms. Adams? What feelings are shown by the worker? Do you think this was a satisfactory termination?

In the sketch above, termination was achieved because of intervention by outside conditions. Termination, like initiation, can also be achieved through conscious planning by either the worker or the client. Ms. Adams might have chosen to discontinue the relationship for a number of reasons that seemed valid to her. She might or might not have decided to let the worker know of this decision. The worker might have been able to arrange for Ms. Adams to receive AFDC, and then to transfer the family to a payments worker, with the worker and Ms. Adams mutually arranging this kind of termination. If clients do not always include workers in their plans for termination, workers must recognize their responsibility to include clients. Since social workers are trained to work *with* their clients rather than *for* them, they will see the termination as a logical step in the planned change process, a contract that the client understands and accepts.

Sometimes before the foreseeable end of the planned change process, unexpected termination may come about, because the worker or client or both leave the area. If the worker leaves the agency, or at least the unit that serves the client, it is important to explain the reasons to the client and to mutually explore the necessary activities to effect a transfer. Perhaps a conference with the new worker can be arranged before the old worker leaves. At least the client must be appraised of the plan and given a chance to communicate his or her feelings. If the client is the one to leave, the worker should indicate the agency's concern by offering to refer the client to another agency, if possible. Sometimes that is not possible, but by the offer the client may be made to feel worth some attention even though no longer around. Perhaps the client will want to call the worker, or write.

Without fostering a sense of dependency, the worker needs to convey a sense of concern. Sometimes, clients simply leave without giving the worker a chance to react. Then the worker must deal with his or her own feelings. It is hard not to feel that the worker is at fault, and perhaps thorough evaluation will reveal some problems that can be avoided in the future.

Any discussion of termination can hardly ignore the need for evaluation. Evaluation of the planned change process must certainly continue on the part of both client and worker all through the effort, to make sure that the original assessment still seems valid, and that they are proceeding along the right track. According to Pincus and Minihan, there are at least two major reasons why the social worker reviews and evaluates the change effort.

> The first has to do with his professional obligation to the client and action system members to indicate to what extent the outcome goals agreed upon in his contract with them have been realized. The credibility of the profession of social work rests on its ability to demonstrate that it can bring about the changes it claims to be able to make. Though this is usually considered to be a research problem, it is not just that. Generalizations about social work intervention must be based on a large number of cases, but it is still necessary to measure change in individual planned change efforts. The better the practitioner does in demonstrating and documenting the results of his work in each case the easier it will be to conduct needed research. Thus the first reason for evaluation and review stems from the fact that the worker is accountable for the results of his planned change effort to the specific client as well as to the general public which supports the profession.
>
> A second reason for the evaluation is that an explicit review and assessment of failures and accomplishments can be a valuable learning experience for those involved in the planned change effort, including the worker. It can help consolidate the lessons learned as a result of going through the planned change effort and can enhance the ability of the client or action system to cope with similar situations in the future. Thus even if mistakes were made and not all the outcome goals were realized, if those involved learned why the goals were not accomplished and how to avoid similar mistakes in the future, the planned change effort will have some payoff.[9]

Other systems

So far, most of the discussion of the casework process has emphasized the change in the client. In an earlier era, this might have been accepted as the total purpose of casework. Now we recognize that some problems are not within the individual, but must be dealt with through other systems. To expect people to adjust to every other system is clearly unrealistic.

William Schwartz, the group worker whom we cited earlier, views the worker in the role of mediator between systems. He sees all systems as mutually interdependent, and therefore sees problems as situations that need mediation between systems.

Clients whose complaints involve other people, institutions, or organizations may have just cause for complaint. Perhaps the landlord *is* making unfair profit on a hapless tenant. Perhaps the teacher *does* have it in for the complaining child. Perhaps the judge *did* impose an unjust sentence. Certainly when we look at the variety and complexity of intersystems relationships, we can hardly assume that our client is always the one who needs to be changed. In fact, when we look at the variety and complexity of intersystems relationships we may be likely to think that everything needs changing except the client. What can be done to help a child from a deprived home? If a black youngster is in trouble with school, police, and juvenile authorities, it is hard to believe that the fault lies with the child entirely. Poverty, poor housing, lack of a role model, institutional racism, lack of motivation, and earlier inadequacies in his background can all be blamed on other systems. The trouble is that the other systems are frequently inaccessible to change. Perhaps the young person has already been sentenced to punishment or committed to treatment. The worker still has the responsibility to listen and encourage, to try to form a warm relationship. From there, the worker's performance of Schwartz's five central tasks becomes crucial in helping the youngster. The first three tasks — searching out common ground, detecting and challenging the obstacles that obscure the common ground, and contributing data, facts, ideas, and value concepts that are not available to the client— all these are real contributions by the worker to a young client who admittedly has many points against him. In addition to providing sympathy and support, the worker is dealing with the very real problems in a realistic way. The fourth task, that of lending a vision to a client, provides a very special dimension to the relationship. The worker whose life experience may or may not be better, but is certainly different from that of the client, can share with the client feelings of individual worth and social good. Finally, the worker can set limits and requirements so that the client can, in this relationship at least, expect consistency. The purpose of all this is to give the client a firm sense of self-determination, even in a limited way. The client will be helped to feel that even though life has not been fair, still he can do something about it, and that he can depend on the worker to help him do something about it.

For most workers, however, reliance on the client's ability to adjust to or make the best of a bad situation will not suffice. Most workers will want to do something to change the systems that contribute to the bad situation. While the worker cannot change everything, it is his or her responsibility to mediate between the client and some parts of the system. The worker probably cannot change the judge's sentence but may be able to talk with the court counselor about this particular judge. Does the judge have some biases that may yield? Is re-election imminent? Is there a movement for reform of the juvenile court system? These are increasingly longer-range goals that may not help this particular client. But workers realize that their efforts on behalf of the client reach far beyond the interview, even beyond the personal relationship. On the other hand, the mediating worker may find that the young person's school is amenable to the suggestion for special tutoring, or even a change of classroom instructors. Maybe bringing the family into the picture—or getting some of them out of it—will help everyone concerned. The point to remember is that many systems are affecting and affected by this individual. Intervention in some systems may help a great deal to straighten out others. Neither worker nor client can effect complete change, but change on a small scale may spread to other systems.

These examples of casework modalities are not exhaustive. They are meant only to show a little of the change and ferment current and traditional in working with individuals. For a more complete account of the current state, students should see *Social Work Treatment*, edited by Francis J. Turner.[10]

Change models in casework

So far we have looked at the steps in the change process and at the systems that may need change or be available for change. Now we need to look very briefly at some of the philosophical bases for bringing about change. As we do this, we must remember that all of the theories and techniques mentioned are eagerly espoused by some worker, particularly by their authors.

Early casework was nearly always a matter of providing urgently needed goods such as food, clothing, a job, or rent money. It is fascinating to read early accounts of the interviews between worker and client. Home visits were the rule, rather than the exception, and workers seem remarkably unselfconscious about giving advice freely and frequently.

As casework became a more sophisticated process, two separate schools of practice emerged. One was called the *diagnostic school* and leaned heavily on stages of human development as explained by Freud. The second was called the *functional school* and emphasized the importance of human and agency functions and their interrelationships. While these differences seem in retrospect to be minor, compared with the amount of personal involvement and skill that every worker uses, still they were important in their time, and whole schools of social work were founded, based on these differing philosophies.

The diagnostic-psychoanalytic school took its cue from the ego psychology writings of Sigmund Freud and later of Erik Erikson, who theorized that every human being goes through certain stages of growth, each of which is vital to overall development. Certain stages are more likely to prove stressful than others, and the lack of resolution of one or more of these stages will prove permanently detrimental. Through long, involved casework, the client may be able to gain insight into the root of difficulty and may eventually be able to understand the need for defenses. Once understood, perhaps defenses will no longer be necessary and can be abandoned.

For example: Ms. Riggs was referred to the medical social worker by her doctor after extensive tests showed no physical basis for her persistent shortness of breath. The worker showed her concern and interest in Ms. Riggs, rather than in her symptoms. She took a rather exhaustive social and family history; that is, she asked Ms. Riggs to tell her about her childhood, her relationships with parents and siblings, about discipline, particularly as it related to toilet training and sex play. She learned that Ms. Riggs had been afraid of her father, particularly after she started to date. He had been very strict about her boyfriends and the hours she kept. Marriage had been a way out, and at first she had been very happy. But Mr. Riggs demanded sexual relations "all the time," and Ms. Riggs found that she was becoming short of breath when he was due home from work. The worker asked if she had ever felt that way before. Ms. Riggs said, with some surprise, that she had felt the same symptoms when her father was waiting for her after a date.

While this is an oversimplification, it does give some picture of what a diagnostic caseworker would do. This model contains many of the basic qualifications of social work, such as acceptance, recognition of individual dignity, and self-determination. Children's relationships with their family are certainly important in determining the kind of adult they will be. But the relationships are interdependent, and ongoing. As children are affected by their parents, so do they affect them. Older brothers and sisters are jealous of younger ones, but so are younger ones jealous of older ones. Furthermore, as people grow, they change, not just through childhood and adolescence, but presumably throughout life till death. Diagnostic thinking must take all systems into account.

A worker of the functional school, on the other hand, would see the client and the client's problem in relation to the agency and its functions. The functional worker would see the client as an independent individual, able to use or discard services offered by the agency.

For example: Mr. Brooks came to the family agency on the advice of his mother-in-law. He and his wife had been having very serious quarrels, and he was afraid she would leave him. The worker was sympathetic and hoped the agency could help. But she wanted Mr. Brooks to understand that it would be necessary to bring his wife, at least to some meetings. Also, appointments would be made once a week for six weeks. After that, both Mr. Brooks and the worker would decide if more time was necessary. Since the agency did not allow home visits, Mr. Brooks would be responsible for getting to the office on time for appointments. In some ways, the functionalists were closer to current schools of reality therapy and behavior modification than to the diagnostic school. Functionalists dealt with the here and now, rather than with the there and then.

Perlman and Hollis are both members of the diagnostic school, and their writings are highly recommended for students interested in pursuing that method. Both writers have become less puristic in recent editions of their basic texts: *Social Casework: A Problem Solving Process* by Perlman, and *Casework: A Psychosocial Therapy* by Hollis. In any event, the dichotomy between the two schools is more interesting historically than currently.

As behavior modification is a method of casework, so is therapy. All casework is not therapy, but therapy is one method used by caseworkers. An example of behavior modification is reality therapy. Reality therapy was introduced by William Glasser, a psychiatrist, who was trained in the psychoanalytic method. His book, *Reality Therapy* (1965), describes his interest in making the client or patient more responsible for his or her own behavior.[11] It rejects the classic concept of mental illness, which supposes that people are not responsible. It considers the conscious mind the only area that can be reached by therapy. However, not only must the individual be conscious, but must also feel that he or she is worthwhile and lovable, that someone cares. This is the basis for reality therapy. The client is living right now in a certain situation that can be affected. The involvement of the worker or therapist is an important aspect. The worker is not removed or objective, but very much concerned with the client. The worker cares and lets the client know that he or she cares—but is *not* interested in excuses or explanations. The worker realizes that the client has had tremendous problems to overcome, but the worker has confidence in the client's ability to overcome them. This method leans heavily on self-determination and assumes a great deal of client responsibility. Glasser—who is the leading proponent—claims to have great success with all kinds of clients.

Here is an example of reality therapy: Kevin arrived for his first appointment with the court counselor. Sulky, but handsome, Kevin said defiantly that he was tired of always being the fall guy. His arrest had been a frame; the cops had it in for him. The counselor responded sympathetically but firmly. Kevin might not like having to report, might not like his job, might not like probation at all. Nevertheless, the court's rule was definite. Kevin was in trouble and what could he do to get out of it? Kevin insisted that it wasn't his fault. The other guys were the troublemakers. He had been the one to get caught. Still sympathetically, the counselor replied that neither he nor Kevin could change the court's ruling, but between them they might be able to give Kevin an easier time the next six months. He emphasized that he was vitally concerned in Kevin's successful probation but said Kevin would be the one to make it successful or unsuccessful. When Kevin fantasized about what he would like to do to the cops, the counselor interrupted, directing Kevin to talk about what he could really do on a job. When Kevin suggested that he might work as a bag boy, the counselor encouraged him to mention possible employers. He suggested that Kevin see the employers on his list before next week and be prepared to report on his job-seeking efforts.

Reality therapy uses many of the casework principles that are applicable to all of social work, and Glasser has been very successful with groups, who support and criticize each other, the same way that the therapist supports and criticizes. Reality therapy is a functional approach.

Behavior modification is a model developed by clinical psychologists. Original work was done by Pavlov, whose dog was presented with food and a ringing bell simultaneously. The food evoked a salivation response. The bell did not. After many repetitions, the dog linked the bell to the food and produced salivation even without the food. This type of conditioning is called *respondent* or *classical*, and depends on the subject's own behavior producing the feedback.

Further work that has been more important to social workers was pioneered by B. F. Skinner and is called *operant conditioning*. Skinner theorized that behavior is controlled by its consequences. If the behavior is rewarded, it will appear more frequently. If it is not reinforced, it will appear less frequently.

> In behavior modification, the main focus is on observable responses, rather than psychic causes. . . . Most behaviorists allege that symptoms are no different from other responses, in that behavior (1) falls predominantly into the respondent or the operant realm, (2) was learned through processes of conditioning, (3) obeys the same laws of learning and conditioning as does so-called normal behavior, and (4) is amenable to change through the careful application of what is known about learning and behavioral modification.[12]

The behaviorist seeks to learn what specific behaviors the client sees as a problem. How often do the behaviors occur? What is the stimulus that elicits the behavior? To determine the answers to these questions, the worker may observe the client in a natural setting, or may accept the client's self-report, or may use some experimental technique to stimulate the natural stimulus-response.

Once the assessment is made, with the client's full participation, techniques for modifying the behavior may be decided upon. Operant conditioning includes positive reinforcement, extinction, differential reinforcement, and response shaping. Behavior modification practitioners are less interested in the reason for behavior than they are in changing it. They are skeptical of the use of insight, and they think that behavior, not intent, is the basis for the well-being of individuals, families, or groups. Some practitioners give rewards for good behavior, while others punish bad behavior. The main thing is that the rewards or punishments be consistently given, so that the subject knows the connection between the behavior and the reward or punishment.

Proponents of this method are enthusiastic about its merits in dealing with clients with varying kinds and degrees of incapacity. They point out its use in working with the developmentally disabled, the emotionally disturbed, normal school children, and mature adults. Furthermore, training workers in this method is relatively simple, so that ward aides, teachers, and prison guards can use the system of rewards or punishment. Its success does not depend on verbal skills of the patient. Finally, they say, it works.

For example: Judy was a developmentally disabled nine-year-old who attended a special class in a large public school. Her behavior prevented her and the other children from concentrating on the work at hand. The teacher initiated the token system, giving each child a token for a finished assignment. At first, Judy received no tokens, while some of the others received three a day. The other children redeemed their tokens for candy at the end of the day. The next day Judy got a token. She was so proud of it that she was reluctant to redeem it.

Those who oppose behavior modification suggest that clients are deprived of their right of self-determination. The treatment takes away their human dignity. The film *Clockwork Orange* is a science fiction example of the kind of abuses that might occur under the use of behavior modification. The film depicts a young man whose sexual behavior is so intolerable that he is given a course in behavior modification that completely alters his personality. Abuses can occur whenever people intervene in other people's lives, and a model cannot be defended or denounced on the basis of possible abuse. Like other models, behavior modification has value in helping people with their

problems. Like other models, it is not a panacea for all kinds of problems.

William J. Reid and Laura Eptein are credited with the development of the model called task-centered treatment.[13] Based on brief,
time-limited casework efforts in the mid-sixties, this model emphasizes the need to focus on at least one problem and at least one task to
be performed by the client. Task-centered treatment emphasizes the
contract as a means for checking on the work being carried on. The
worker's acceptance of the client as a person who can make responsible decisions and follow through on them is basic to the model as to
all models; but the task is the focus.

Summary

Social casework is one kind of intervention used by social workers. It
employs the planned change process, and deals mainly with individuals in a one-to-one relationship. The interview is the usual method
of communication, and the establishment of a relationship is followed
by the making of a contract. The worker and client work together toward the solution of the problem and, eventually, the relationship is
terminated by mutual consent.

Some of the more recent methods of intervention are based on the
earlier efforts of social workers to practice different philosophies. Reality therapy and behavior modification are examples of methods that
can be used with individuals, families, groups, and communities.

Notes

1. Helen H. Perlman, *Social Casework: A Problem Solving Process* (Chicago:
University of Chicago Press, 1967), p. 9.

2. Perlman, *Social Casework*, p. 10.

3. Florence Hollis, *Casework: A Psychosocial Therapy* (New York: Random
House, 1972), p. 10.

4. Felix P. Biestek, *The Casework Relationship* (Chicago: Loyola University
Press, 1957), p. 17.

5. Perlman, *Social Casework*, p. 25.

6. Alfred Kadushin, *The Social Work Interview* (New York: Columbia University Press, 1972).

7. William Schwartz, "The Social Worker in the Group," *Social Welfare Forum* (1961), p. 157.

8. Lawrence Shulman, *A Casebook of Social Work with Groups: The Mediating Model* (New York: Council on Social Work Education, 1968), p. 67.

9. Allen Pincus and Anne Minihan, *Social Work Practice* (Itasca, Ill.: F. E. Peacock Publishers, 1973), pp. 273–74.

10. Francis J. Turner, *Social Work Treatment* (New York: Macmillan, 1974).

11. William Glasser, *Reality Therapy* (New York: Harper & Row, 1985).

12. Edwin J. Thomas, "Social Casework and Social Group Work: The Behavioral Approach," in *The Encyclopedia of Social Work*, vol. 2 (New York: National Association of Social Workers, 1971), pp. 1226–27.

13. William J. Reid and Laura Eptein, *Task Centered Casework* (New York: Columbia University Press, 1972).

5

SOCIAL WORK WITH
FAMILIES

Social work with individuals is known as casework and usually involves a worker and one client. But as we see in Chapter 5, individuals can rarely be considered by themselves. For most people, the system with which they are most closely related is the family. Caseworkers have always known this, and nearly all caseworkers take the family into account, either personally or indirectly, when they work with an individual.

What is a family? Basically, it is a small, primary, face-to-face group. It is also a social system of considerable complexity and tremendous importance in human life. As we saw in Chapter 2 on social systems, each individual is dependent on and depended on by other individuals. In a nuclear family, the name given to parents and their children in one household, the interdependence is very intimate indeed. The family system is living proof that a change in a subsystem causes change in all parts of the larger system; while a change in the larger system causes change in all the subsystems. Add to this the obvious fact that families are always in the process of change, and we see that families must be constantly in the process of adjusting to a new homeostasis. Sometimes the adjustments are helpful and useful; sometimes they are not.

The whole process of input, processing, output, and feedback is enormously important in a family system. As we will see, Virginia Satir theorizes that all families have communication systems. Murray Bowen found all families produce members who behave in similar ways. Jay Haley has learned all family members learn their own roles as members of that family. Sometimes these communications, prod-

74

ucts, and roles are conscious and intended. Sometimes they are not. The task of the social worker is to try to help family members become conscious of their identities and try to help the process work better. Family members may be related by blood or by marriage, or, we must now recognize, may not have any formal relationship. Traditionally, the family's functions have been to develop its members socially, physically, and emotionally. Even in informal, unrelated groups, these functions are viewed as necessary and desirable and are carried on to some extent. The family system is, therefore, a link between the individual system and the larger society and, as such, it merits attention from anyone who is interested in social services.

Recently social workers have found themselves challenged by more and different kinds of family configurations. The traditional, two-parent-and-children picture is complex. How much more complex, then, is the family with one parent? This parent may be father or mother. The dissolution of the marriage may have been eagerly sought or reluctantly tolerated by the various family members. In other families, there may not be a formal marriage, but rather a couple living together, whose legal rights are tenuous indeed.

Still another type of family we now recognize is that of two people of the same sex living together in a close relationship with the same kinds of communicaton and role problems that we have seen in traditional families. All of these are systems needing intervention in much the same way as the traditional family. Here the attitude of the worker assumes even greater importance. Nearly everyone is in favor of families. But not everyone can or does accept the idea of some of the newer lifestyles or the new combinations of people known as families. The social worker must be very conscious and aware of himself or herself. Biestek's principles must again be brought into use. Being accepting and nonjudgmental of an abusing stepparent may not be easy. But the social worker's inputs, whether positive or negative, will be very important to the family. We saw in Chapter 1 that knowledge, skills, and values are all involved in a worker's efforts to help a family.

Social work with families is particularly concerned with the initiation stage of the planned change process. Because of the many people involved, perception of the need for change may be uneven. For example, a woman who is also a wife and mother may be ready to ask for help with her family's problem. The husband-father may be unwilling or unable to do so. Perhaps a teacher or a school social worker sees problems from the child's viewpoint. Getting the parents to share this perception may be quite a challenge. In working with families as in working with other client systems, the worker starts where the client is, working with as many family members as the worker can reach, effecting those changes that are possible and necessary. The family worker, like the caseworker, must distinguish between families who actually want intervention and those who have intervention thrust upon them. The worker must also recognize and act on the difference between supportive and insight intervention. The three major approaches to family therapy described in this chapter are primarily designed for those families actively seeking help, though their theories and skills can be incorporated in work with families less motivated.

Ms. Brown had been invited to talk with the school social worker about her son Terry's frequent absences from school. Hesitantly at first, then in a rush, Ms. Brown described her efforts to keep her job as a clerk typist in spite of the illnesses of her younger child, Steve. She confessed that she knew Terry should not be missing school but that seemed better than her missing work. With some bitterness she described her financial and emotional difficulties, including her relationship with the boys' father. The social worker listened sympathetically, commented that Ms. Brown certainly had many things to worry about, and asked if she had considered taking her troubles to a family agency. Ms. Brown did not know about such an agency, but she said she would like some help from someone.

Do you think Ms. Brown saw her family as candidates for family therapy? Do you think school social workers are likely to offer family therapy?

Just as some individuals are better able than others to cope with life's problems and tasks, so are some families better able to cope. First of all, members of the family must be able to function as individuals, and then in their roles as members of the family. Second, they must be able to cope, both as individuals and as family members, with the demands made by larger systems. For example, a man must have a feeling of his own worth, but this is related to his worth as a husband, a father, an employee, and a wage earner. If there were one prescribed measure of performance, this would be difficult enough, but the rules keep changing. Men who were brought up to be hard-working and thrifty, to support their families and "get ahead," may find that society—or their own children—do not accord them the honor and respect that they feel is their due. Other men, because of race, lack of education, lack of motivation, or some other reason may be unable or unready to work steadily and be good providers. As they grow older, both kinds of men may feel that they should get more from life and seek ways to do so.

Women have a need to respect themselves as individuals, as wives, mothers, employees or employers, and/or wage earners, but not necessarily in that order. For them, too, the rules keep changing. A woman who was brought up to be a wife and mother may find that she is neither or that she is both, but in the latter case her children—and the larger society—are unimpressed with these achievements.

Children also have problems of coping with drastic changes, but for them the demands and their responses to the demands come faster and change oftener as they grow and change. And these problems relate not only to members of the nuclear family. Those faced by grandparents, in-laws, siblings, aunts, and uncles are equally bewildering.

Such discontinuities and role confusions are obvious in white middle-class America, but they are equally important in poverty areas and especially black poverty areas. A stereotype of black matriarchal society has been accepted as a basic difference, though studies have indicated that in many black families a strong, authoritative father is the norm. Strong mothers have been forced into the role because of poverty or the father's lack of education, rather than because of race. If black women have been better able to get the available jobs than black men, the reason seems to be the faulty organization of the larger system rather than any intrinsic difference in black and white culture.

Chicano families have been described by quite a different set of stereotypes, including such ideas as "family centered," "familistic," "extended family," "paternalistic," and "male dominated." In "The Chicano Family: A Review of Research," by Miguel Montiel, some of the sweeping generalizations have been discounted and others tempered. Montiel's conclusion seems to be that Chicano families, like most others in our culture, are in the process of change, that broad generalizations about them are likely to be invalid, and that, most of all, a focus on pathology rather than diversity and strengths is mistaken.[1]

Of all systems, perhaps the family is the one in which the complex interrelationships are most obvious. Family relationships start earlier and last longer than nearly any other. They are also apt to be the closest, the most demanding, and the most rewarding. It is not surprising, then, that social workers and other professionals have considered the family worthy of a variety of kinds of intervention.

Efforts at prevention of the worst kinds of family problems have long been made by social workers, psychologists, and home economists, as well as lawyers, doctors, and the clergy. Education for parenthood, for money management, for sexual expertise has been attempted both formally and informally. Perhaps some of it has been worthwhile. There is no way to know how many families are still intact as a result of these efforts. Certainly, prevention is easier and less expensive than treatment or rehabilitation, and well worth the effort.

Efforts at providing services that the family may need but may be unable to provide for itself have been made by social workers since the days of the friendly visitors. These visitors were well-meaning upper-class men and women who sought to give both goods and services to people less well off, as we saw in Chapter 3. Social workers provided food, shelter, and clothing for many kinds of families whose own resources were sorely limited. Provision was necessary because of lacks in the here and now. Other resources, such as employment, medical care, and counseling services have also been made available to families in need of them. Because of the nature of family relationships, these services can hardly be proffered to one member of the family without involving some of the others.

All the points made concerning relationships with an individual hold true for relationships between worker and family. Sometimes, the worker does not plan to involve the family, but when a home visit or an office appointment is made, the worker finds that he or she is talking with the whole family.

For example: The Red Cross home service worker called on the mother of a young sailor whose hand had been accidentally cut off in heavy machinery. The worker was not looking forward to the interview, but mentally reviewed the words she would use in breaking the news. When she arrived at the home, she found the mother, father, younger brother, and fiancée assembled. Realizing nothing could be gained from delay, she told them immediately. As they reacted to the news, they turned to each other for comfort and support. The worker could only feel relieved that she was not the only one with the mother.

The family, then, needs both preventive and provisive services. It also needs rehabilitative services when the family structure or function fails.

Since the early 1950s, some psychiatrists, psychologists, sociologists, and social workers have emphasized family therapy. Advocates of family therapy see the family as the most important of all systems and regard individuals as subsystems who are interdependent and symbiotic on each other and on the family as a unit.

While social work has always been aware of the effect of the family on an individual, the emphasis in family therapy is on the family rather than the individual. In 1956 Murray Bowen, a psychiatrist with the National Institutes of Health, studied the families of schizophrenics. He concluded that it was the schizophrenic family that produced schizophrenic children. As a result of his investigation, he observed that "the family is a system in that change in one part of the system is followed by compensatory change in other parts." Later, he stated, "The family is a number of different kinds of systems. It can accurately be designated as a social system, a cultural system, a games system, a communications system, or any of several other designations."[2]

Social workers in family therapy operate in the same sequence of planned change as caseworkers, group workers, or community workers. First, someone must feel a need for change, someone must initiate the change, the change relationship must be established, a contract made, and the change begun, generalized, and stabilized, and finally the relationship must be terminated. But the process is more complex in that the family, rather than an individual member, is the client. In the first phase—recognition of need for change—it is rarely a family recognition by the whole family that all members need help. More likely, one member is the recognized problem, and only after a series of sessions does the family see that all need help.

Given the basic orientation of the family as the unit in need of help, there are various philosophies as to how the help can best be given. In 1969 the Regional Rehabilitation Research Institute of the University of Washington School of Social Work published the results of an investigation of the family as a unit of study and treatment. This extensive investigation of the literature on family therapy classified three main styles of methods of work with families. They are psychoanalytic, integrative, and communicative-interactive. Like the casework methodologies, each category has its own proponents, who, on the basis of their professional background and experience, defend each category at the expense of the others.[3]

Psychoanalytic approach

Family therapists of the psychoanalytic school operate on the same premises as diagnostic caseworkers of Freudian persuasion. They believe in the need for insight into an unconscious mental life by both client and therapist, and in the predetermined development of the individual. According to this theory, every human being goes through predictable phases of the oral, anal, oedipal, latency, adolescent, and adult periods before reaching maturity.

In the oral stage, infants learn to satisfy their need, both sexual and aggressive, through their mouths. Babies cry, suck, and eventually coo and speak through their mouths. Food and attention come as a result of exercising their mouths. In the anal stage, children learn to enjoy the experience of owning or withholding their feces. Again this is a way of getting attention from the mother. In the oedipal stage, regarded by some psychoanalysts as the most crucial, children learn to internalize the position of parents and other family members. They must accept the father as the mother's sex partner and recognize that the children's positions are quite different. By this time, according to Freudian theory, children are learning to distinguish between their own natural drives and the demands made by others, mainly their parents. They must reconcile their own sexual-aggressive urges, their libidos, with the demands of reality as imposed by their parents, who represent their superegos.

When the conflicts brought about by these forces (libido and superego) are not resolved at any stage, the result is neurosis. If the conflicts are satisfactorily resolved, the result is a healthy functioning ego. The latter is the goal of psychoanalytic treatment. Since neuroses always have their roots in childhood, psychoanalysis attempts to uncover material that has been repressed, and therefore relegated to the unconscious. The patient divulges material from the past, through memories, dreams, or free association, and the analyst helps the patient to understand and work through the previously unresolved conflict. Conflict is not the cause of neurosis; only the lack of resolution of conflict is.

The family, especially the mother, is seen as having tremendous impact at each stage in an individual's life; and, therefore, the family is seen as a natural starting point for the practice of psychoanalytic therapy. However, the most important emphasis is on the unconscious fantasies of the child, not the family as it really was. Thus the interaction of the family as it could be observed by a therapist is less important to the psychoanalyst than are the internalized representations as reported by the patient in therapy.

Two of the major proponents of psychoanalytic therapy, Ivan Boszormenyi-Nagy and James L. Framo, wrote the book *Intensive Family Therapy* in which they state their belief that they must distinguish between intensive and supportive therapy.[4] Their preference is for intensive therapy, and this typically involves work by one or more therapists with a family over a period of several years. The emphasis is on the individual's neuroses and their roots in the past.

When the focus is on family communication, attention is given primarily to the psychological level and unconscious communication. Psychoanalytic practitioners vary in their approaches. Some prefer individual interviews, some prefer to intersperse these with family interviews, and some prefer to see groups of unrelated individuals having similar neuroses. What they share is an effort to get at the family's problems through intensive work in the psychological background of each individual.

For example: Mr. Wright called for an appointment with a social worker who had been recommended to him by a co-worker in the bank where Mr. Wright worked. Mr. Wright explained that his family seemed to him totally lacking in family communication. He rarely saw his two teenage sons, his wife talked to him about only the most superficial things, and he came home at night too tired to do more than watch television as he ate his dinner and then go to bed. He made a good salary, provided a good home, and did not think he was getting his money's worth from his family. He wondered if the agency could do anything for him. The worker hoped that the family could be helped, but asked if the Wrights were all interested in doing something about their situation and suggested that a series of weekly meetings be set up, with various members seen on different days. When he heard that the process would probably take three or four years, Mr. Wright said he thought he should think the matter over.

Do you think the worker should have started the interview differently? Would you see the Wright's problem as one that would lend itself to psychoanalytic study? Why?

Integrative approach

The integrative approach is an effort to include both the individual and the family in diagnosis and treatment. Its major concept is that of *role*. In every family, different individuals play different roles. In addition to the obvious ones—mother, father, oldest, youngest, daughter, son—individual families specify which members will have conflicting or complementary roles. Helen H. Perlman, explaining role, says, "Role offers a social-functioning focus which embraces people in interaction. . . . Role does not allow us to get lost in personality *per se* . . . most persons know and assess themselves only through their role performance."[5]

Otto Pollack, a sociologist who has written about role theory, says, "Family members are viewed as one another's reciprocal and preferred need-satisfiers."[6] He sees the family as standing between the individual and the more complex organization of society. Nathan Ackerman, a psychiatrist, sees three levels of phenomena in the interaction between an individual and a group: (1) the structure of the environment; (2) interpersonal relationships; and (3) the internal organization of personalities. He sees the concept of social role as a bridge between the processes of intrapsychic life and social participation. The purpose of the family, he thinks, is security, survival, sexual union and fulfillment, the care of the young and the aged, the cultivation of bonds of affection and identity, and training for social participation.[7] According to him, breakdown may come at any level of interaction, but his therapeutic approach is primarily to the family unit; the individual and his or her psyche is secondary. Ackerman and his colleagues wish to include in the family sessions all members of the nuclear family, as well as important grandparents, and even pets. However, they will also see individual members or subgroups when this seems indicated, so that their mode of operation is quite flexible. One problem with this flexibility is that training and education of the therapist is difficult. Therapists depend on personal innovations and must be able to assimilate completely the many theories about values, mental health, and human growth. Arthur L. Leader, a social worker, suggests that the therapist's intervention must be vigorous and active, as opposed to the psychoanalytic aloofness and lack of involvement. Because some families' interactive patterns are so strong, the therapist may be sucked into their patterns and experience the same feelings of hopelessness that they suffer.

Proponents of the integrative approach need broad knowledge and highly developed skills, as well as values that are strong and sure. Just as with individuals, families need support and understanding, and the benefit of the worker's experience. Schwartz's five central tasks, listed in Chapter 4, are applicable to work with families.

For example: Mr. Wright came to the family agency by prearranged appointment. He had with him his wife and two sons. Mrs. Wright and the boys sat on the sofa in the worker's office. Mr. Wright took a straight chair off to the side. When the worker asked if everyone knew why they had come to the office, Mr. Wright began a fairly detailed explanation of events leading to his call. His wife and sons sat quietly, neither agreeing nor disagreeing. When he finished, the worker asked Mrs. Wright if this was the way it seemed to her. She looked startled at being questioned directly and said she guessed so. One of the boys said no one had told him why they were coming. The other boy looked annoyed.

What do you think the worker might have guessed about this family in this short time? Why didn't the worker let the father do all the talking for the family? Would you have thought anything about the seating arrangement?

Communicative-interactive approach

Conjoint family therapy is the outstanding example of the communicative-interactive approach. The main concept of this type of therapy is that all family communication involves a multiplicity of messages at one time. Actually, this is true of all communication, in or out of the family. Because communication is so important in this kind of therapy, the therapist tries very early to find out what kinds of messages are being given in a particular family. According to Don Jackson and Virginia Satir, parents are the models for the kind of communication that children give and receive.[8] If parental communication is faulty, it is probably a result of *their* parents having poor communication. This would indicate that communicative-interactive therapy is not so completely concerned with the here and now as it would seem to be.

The second major concept involves the idea of family homeostasis. This is an example of the homeostasis or balance in any system. A change in one part of the system causes a change in other parts. If an individual changes as a result of therapy, the rest of the family will change—change, not necessarily improve. The only way to replace the lost homeostasis is with a new, more satisfactory balance. Because so much dysfunctional behavior is bound up with double messages, according to this theory, the therapist's job is to serve as a model for good communication. The therapist must first clarify the communication between family members, then send the therapist's messages clearly. Unfortunately, the family may not appreciate having defenses broken down; particularly they may not like having the onus removed from the "problem member," whom Satir calls the "identified patient."[9]

The therapist takes a rather strong position, getting information from each member of the family to recognize the kinds of interaction in this particular family and then making direct suggestions for change. For example, members of the family may not speak *for* each other or *about* each other. They may speak *to* each other.

This approach to family therapy is readily learned by members of various professions: social workers, psychologists, communications analysts, and doctors, among others. According to its proponents, basic changes in family communications can take place in a matter of a few months.

For example: The Wright family filed into the interviewing room. As his wife and sons seated themselves, Mr. Wright launched into an explanation of the behavior of his younger son that had brought the family to the office. Jack had been reported by his school as a truant, and there was some suspicion that he had been pilfering change from the school milk fund. Mr. Wright expressed his anger and disappointment with Jack, saying that the boy never appreciated all his father did for him. The worker turned to Jack, asking for his version of the story. Mrs. Wright answered that Jack never seemed to care for the family or their worry about him. The worker again asked Jack how it seemed to him. Jack said his parents had already told the story. The worker said she would like to hear how Jack felt. With tears in his eyes, Jack began to explain.

In this example, who is the identified patient? Do you think the worker knew enough about the problem to ask Jack immediately for his story? How do you think the rest of the family would react to this?

Compared with social casework, family therapy is a new way of trying to help people. Its methods are not too different from casework methods, and the basic knowledge, skills, and values of all social work and vitally important in working with families. Some of family therapy is used by many caseworkers, and family therapists practice some casework.

Where families are intact, working with the family is desirable and helpful. Unfortunately, many families are not intact. Many individuals have no families or no families with whom they interact. Even the most enthusiastic proponent of family therapy recognizes that the family is only one of innumerable systems encountered by an individual and that, in some cases, the family is not there at all. Still, if family therapy is not a solution to all social problems, it is one more way of looking at and attacking some social problems.

An excellent casebook for family therapy is *Techniques of Family Therapy* by Jay Haley and Lynn Hoffman.[10] In 1985 L'Abate published a two-volume book, *Handbook of Family Psychology and Therapy*.[11] This collection of readings in family therapy is a welcome addition to the literature. However, the thesis of the work is that all theories derive basically from psychoanalysis, behaviorism, and humanism. Students interested in these theories should read this book.

Summary

Social work with families is closely related to casework, but is also closely related to family therapy as carried on by members of other helping professions, including psychiatry and psychology. Family therapy focuses on the family as a system, and proposes the thesis that healthy families produce healthy individuals, and vice versa. Like casework, family therapy uses different methods, and the proponents of each method, on the basis of their own background and experience, defend that method against all others.

Notes

1. Miguel Montiel, "The Chicano Family: A Review of Research," *Social Work* 18, no. 2 (March 1973), pp. 22–30.

2. Murray Bowen, "A Family Concept of Schizophrenia," in *The Etiology of Schizophrenia*, ed. Don Jackson (New York: Basic Books, 1960), p. 353.

3. Joan Stein et al., *The Family as a Unit of Study and Treatment* (Regional Rehabilitation Research Institute, University of Washington, 1969).

4. Ivan Boszormenyi-Nagy and James L. Framo, *Intensive Family Therapy: Theoretical and Practical Aspects* (New York: Harper & Row, 1965).

5. Helen H. Perlman, "The Role Concept and Social Casework: Some Exploration," *Social Service Review* 25 (December 1961), pp. 371–81; and Perlman, *Social Service Review* pp. 17–31.

6. Otto Pollack, "A Family Diagnosis Model," *Social Service Review* 34 (March 1960), pp. 19–31.

7. Nathan Ackerman, *The Psychodynamics of Family Life: Diagnosis and Treatment of Family Relationships* (New York: Basic Books, 1958).

8. Stein, *The Family*, p. 49.

9. Virginia Satir, *Conjoint Family Therapy* (Palo Alto, Calif.: Science and Behavior Books, 1968).

10. Jay Haley and Lynn Hoffman, *Techniques of Family Therapy* (New York: Basic Books, 1967).

11. Luciano L'Abate, *Handbook of Family Psychology and Therapy* (2 vols.) (Chicago: Dorsey Press, 1985).

6

SOCIAL WORK WITH GROUPS

Social casework and social work with families are alike in that they deal with people in already existing relationships. Both these methods recognize the importance of the group to an individual. Belonging to a group is an integral part of life for most people. Sociologists and psychologists have studied the group, and social workers have specialized in this method of working with people.

Social work with groups, like social work with individuals, proceeds through a series of stages. The initial phase may be instigated by the individual group member, a person significant to the member, or by the agency sponsoring the group. In each case someone perceives a need for change. The change may be increased social ability, improved functioning, or a combination of these as described in the following group work model.

Following the initial phase, groups follow a fairly predictable pattern. While members are becoming acquainted with each other and the group leader, they make "polite" conversation. As they get down to the work of the group, they grow less polite, more confrontative, and as each perceives the role he or she is to play in the group, some conflict may break out. Such conflict is not a negative event, but rather an indication that the group is indeed working. If the leader is ready and able to handle it, conflict can start important change; trust among members involves being able to trust all members, even the ones who don't agree.

Group work models

A group can be defined very simply as two or more individuals who have something in common and who interact with each other. Sociologists have classified groups as *primary* and *secondary*. A primary group is one in which members have a face-to-face relationship. A secondary group is one in which the members have only intermittent contacts, and an impersonal relationship. Michael Olmsted, author of *The Small Group,* says:

> a group, then, may be defined as a plurality of individuals who are in contact with one another, who take one another into account, and who are aware of some significant commonality.
>
> An essential feature of a group is that its members have something in common and that they believe that what they have in common makes a difference.[1]

He says the term *small group* is "a neutral, indeed a colorless one —it does not prejudge whether the group in question is operating as a primary or a secondary one."[2] Primary groups are usually small, but small groups are not always primary.

The obvious example of a primary group is the family, which fills the qualification of being face to face and sharing something in common. Many families, however, are not primary groups, for various reasons having to do with time, geographical distance, or lack of interest.

If a natural group, such as a family, is not necessarily a primary group, the corollary is true. It is possible to create a primary group for a specific purpose. It is possible to bring together a group of people with similar needs or problems, and to involve them with each other so that they recognize each other as significant, important people. That is what social group workers do. Sometimes the group worker, as an agent of the agency, forms the group. Sometimes, the group forms itself for its own purpose. Sometimes, the group is formed as a combined effort by the individuals involved and the agency.

Social workers recognize at least three models of group work. Papell and Rothman, in their article "Social Group Work Models: Possession and Heritage," list social goals, and remedial and reciprocal models.[3]

Social goals model

Early group work, like early casework, emphasized a strong direction on the part of the worker and a strong feeling that the worker—or the agency as represented by the worker—knew the right answers. Early group work agencies included neighborhood houses, settlements, the YMCA, Girl Scouts, and Boy Scouts. All of these agencies shared the purpose of making better citizens of the members. Settlement and neighborhood houses were instituted in areas where the poor, and particularly the immigrant poor, lived. The agency provided a haven from the very bad housing, but more than that, it provided an opportunity for people to learn along with their friends and neighbors some of the accepted ways of behaving in a new country. This character-building effort was similar to that of the early caseworkers who gave advice to individuals and families, who were presumed to receive it gratefully. Neighborhood and settlement houses met a real need, and in many places they are still meeting the need to help individuals to adjust to a new system through groups of people like themselves. The group acted as a link between the individual and the larger community. In the early days, the larger community was seen to be "right," and learning and adjusting had to be done mainly by the individual with the assistance of the agency. At the same time that these people were learning to work together, they were becoming socially active. They were able to affect factory working conditions and the political process in their wards, thus changing the larger system. Citizen education and social reform were thus seen as two important results of the settlement movement. The degree to which these results became reality depended to some extent on the degree of involvement by the group, the knowledge and skills of the group leader, and the type of cause on which they chose to work. All settlement groups were not successful, but many served to dispel the alienation of immigrant or other such groups.

Girl Scouts and Boy Scouts had much the same purpose, as did the public schools. The group or the troop or the class was formed to further the aims of the larger society. Group pressure was found to be a valuable aid to authority, whether of society, school, or agency. If you think of your own experience, you will recognize that many of the people who have been effective in socializing you have been members of your peer group, not parents or teachers. The earliest kind of group work, then, espoused *social goals* as its purpose. This is a purpose that still holds today. The number of clubs, groups, and troops have proliferated steadily, attracting more and more members of all ages, sexes, and interests. Among early social workers who wrote and practiced group work of this kind were Gisela Konopka, Grace Coyle, and Gertrude Wilson. They saw the worker's role as that of enabler or teacher. According to Catherine Papell and Beulah Rothman, the key concepts of social goals are social consciousness and social responsibility.

As previously stated, social goals were the first to be considered in the practice of group work. Group work was recognized as a reasonable way of achieving those goals, not only by social workers but by recreation workers and teachers as well. According to Papell and Rothman:

> a serious shortcoming of the social goals model is that it has not produced a theoretical design that is adequate to meet the problems facing practitioners in all areas of service. Its under-emphasis on individual dynamics and its lack of attention to a wide range of individual needs leave the practitioner without guidelines for carrying out a social work function with client groups where individual problems take precedence over societal problems. It is difficult to see how this model would serve (except by distortion) to provide a basis for social group work practice with *admission* or *discharge* groups in a mental hospital.[4]

Even the public schools, with their emphasis on grading and conformity, have not been successful in molding all kinds of children into the exemplary citizens hoped for by parents and teachers. Rules and regulations appeal to some, but not all, children. The efforts of group leaders and teachers are in no way to be denigrated, but some other methods must be recognized in dealing with all kinds of people.

For example: The boy's club meeting was late getting started because Fred and Jim did not come in from the playground but continued their game. John, the president, called the meeting to order, but Fred had not appeared to take minutes. Bill, a younger member, suggested that the group impose a fine on members who came late to meetings. A vote was taken and passed, seven to three. When Fred and Jim came running into the room, they were informed that they must pay a 10-cent fine. Jim flushed and said angrily that it wasn't fair to vote before he and Fred came in—the others knew they were coming. The group leader pointed out that they knew when the meeting began, and that the majority of those present had agreed on a fine. Jim said he would not be part of such a crooked club. He was resigning. He stalked out.

Do you see the group leader in a very strong position? Do you think he was a social worker? How could the situation have been handled? Did you ever have a similar experience, as a member of a group? How did you feel about it?

Remedial model

Group work with a treatment emphasis follows a remedial model. Someone needs a remedy for something not quite right, and the group worker sets out to remedy the situation. This model is closely associated with the casework method. The treatment of the individual is seen as the most important goal. Fritz Redl, a psychiatrist, pioneered in the group treatment of institutionalized children. Robert Vinter is the social worker who is recognized as the leading theoretician for this model. Both Redl and Vinter are concerned with the process of forming the group. Group formation is the first stage in this type of planned change. The worker selects group members whom he or she sees as most likely to fit into a group because of their age, sex, interest, or problem. As the person who forms the group, the worker knows something of the background of each prospective group member, and relies on his or her professional judgment as to who should be in the group. The worker's role is that of expert and change agent rather than enabler or mediator. According to Arthur Blum:

> A "good" group is the group which permits and fosters the growth of its members. This does not presuppose any fixed structure or level of function as being desirable except as it affects the members. . . . Evaluation of the desirability of its [the group's] structure and processes can only be made in relation to the desirability of its effects upon the members and the potential it provides for the worker's information.[5]

With this emphasis, the term *remedial* is readily understood. The group is to serve as a remedy for the various members of it. Konopka says:

the group worker is neither "permissive" nor authoritarian-directive. Acceptance and limit-setting are not considered contradictory in the use of the group work method, but are used according to the assessment of the group members' needs and the situation in which they find themselves.[6]

But acceptance and limit-setting assume a knowledge of and skill in what to accept and where to set limits. In all kinds of group therapy, the worker must emphasize his knowledge and his concern for each person in the group. According to Papell and Rothman, the group leader:

uses a problem-solving approach. . . . He is characteristically directive and assumes a position of clinical preeminence and authority. . . . While his authority must be confirmed by the group, it is not fundamentally established by the group. From this position of authority his intervention may be designed to do *for* the client, as well as *with* the client. The model does not require the worker to give priority to the establishment of group autonomy nor to the perpetuation of the group as a self-help system.[7]

The worker is clearly the expert.

Because of the heavy emphasis on the individual, much of the worker's expert knowledge is in the areas of individual psychology and treatment. The remedial model emphasizes "treatment goals" as diagnosed, assessed, and planned by the worker—not the group.

Vinter has outlined the following principles for social work practice.

1. Specific treatment goals must be established for each member of the client group.

2. The worker attempts to define group purposes so that they are consistent with the several treatment goals established for the individual members.

3. The worker helps the group to develop that system of norms and values that is in accord with the worker's treatment goals.

4. The worker prestructures the content for group sessions based on the worker's knowledge of individuals expressed through his treatment goals as well as his knowledge of structural characteristics and processes that take place within the group.[8]

The remedial group worker, then, forms the group or initiates the change, though the client or some third person may have been the one to feel the need for change. In the other steps of planned change —that is, establishing the relationship, examining alternatives, putting the change behavior into action—the worker is the main figure. The group is seen as the tool for bringing change about. What sorts of groups lend themselves to this directive, authoritarian treatment? As Papell and Rothman suggest, mental hospital patients are one example. According to Papell and Rothman, too:

> the remedial model seems to require a structured institutional context. It assumes clearly defined agency policy in support of treatment goals . . . the remedial model makes less provision for adapting service to the informal life style of the client. It appears to depart from the tradition that the group worker engages with people where he finds them as they go about the business of daily living.[9]

For example: Dr. Jones looked straight at Gary. "Do you want us to believe that you honestly didn't know the other guys in the car were smoking pot when you got in?" Several members of the group groaned. "We can't help you much if you don't level with us, can we, group?" Other members of the group nodded. When Gary spoke, it was to Dr. Jones.

If the social goals model emphasizes the importance of the individual conforming to the larger society, the remedial model emphasizes and uses the group to further the goals of the individual.

Reciprocal model

The third model described by Papell and Rothman is called reciprocal because it assumes a reciprocal relationship between the group and the individual. This is the model described by William Schwartz as the mediating model. According to this theory, the individual and the group are interdependent and the worker is the mediator, not only between the individual and the group, but also between the small group and the larger group or community. In the worker's role of mediator, the client is seen as neither the individual nor the group nor society, but as a dynamic interaction among all three. Schwartz describes this as:

> a relationship between the individual and his nurturing group which we would describe as "symbiotic," each needing the other for his own

life and growth, and each reaching out to the other with all the strength it can command at a given moment.[10]

Schwartz proposes that the social worker avoid seeking his identification from either the needs of the individual or society. Instead, his professional identification would derive from the point at which these two sets of needs converge.

This view of the worker's role is more analogous with our view of social systems than either of the earlier models. The worker who identifies with neither society nor the individual, but tries to see both in their context at a given time, has a broad view of the system. According to Papell and Rothman:

> the repicrocal model has no therapeutic ends, no political or social change problems, to which it is addressed. It is only from the encounter of the individuals that compose a reciprocal group system that direction or problem is determined. Emphasis is placed on engagement in the process of interpersonal relations. It is from this state of involvement that members may call upon each other in their own or a common cause.[11]

In practice, this means to the group worker that the goals that individuals have for themselves become one with the group goals, and that neither of these is set or determined by the worker, whose job is that of mediator. Instead, the group process works to keep worker, individual, group, in step with each other.

Schwartz has given useful listings of the practical tasks with which the mediating worker must cope. They are:

1.   The task of searching out the common ground between the client's perception of his own need and the aspects of social demand with which he is faced.

2.   The task of detecting and challenging the obstacles which obscure the common ground and frustrate the efforts of people to identify their own self-interest with that of their "significant others."

3.   The task of contributing data—ideas, facts, and value-concepts—which are not available to the client and which may prove useful to him in attempting to cope with that part of social reality which is involved in the problems on which he is working.

4.   The task of "lending a vision" to the client in which the worker both reveals himself as one whose own hopes and aspirations are strongly invested in the interaction between people and society and

projects a deep feeling for that which represents individual well-being and the social good.

5. The task of defining the requirements and the limits of the situation in which the client-worker system is set. These rules and boundaries establish the context for the "working contract" which binds the client and the agency to each other and which creates the conditions under which both client and worker assume their respective functions.[12]

All of these tasks are applicable to the group worker, for whom, indeed, they were outlined. The emphasis on a systems orientation makes less important the setting or the kind of group composition than does the emphasis in either the social goals or the remedial models. The important concept in this model is the here and now, and the various systems who are involved in that group. There are numerous examples, of course. Here is one:

> As the ladies trooped into the dayroom, some of them smiled and spoke to the worker; others did not. Some of them greeted others; some did not. Their average age was 69 years. All of them lived in a four-block area, but they were not neighbors in a neighborly sense. When they had seated themselves, the worker began to speak, telling them how pleased she was to see so many there. She did not mention that twice as many had been invited. She explained that since so many people enjoyed meals on wheels, the agency had thought that perhaps they would enjoy each other's company or would like to get together occasionally to talk over problems. The agency was concerned about other things than meals and hoped that the ladies would see some purpose in getting together. A large, white-haired woman said that she thought the meeting was for the purpose of discussing how to lower the cost of the meals. That was what she had come for. Another woman said she thought the group should discuss the question of late meals and incompetent volunteers. At this point, several women spoke at once, both agreeing and contradicting. The worker, raising her voice slightly, explained that the agency had not seen this as the point of the meeting but since there was so much interest, perhaps this would be a good starting point.

Which of the five tasks can you see in practice in this example? At which stage of the change process do you see this group? What factors in group composition seem important? What do you think the group leader was trying to do? What do you think she should be doing?

With regard to social group work models, we can say that the social goals model seeks the good of the group; the remedial model seeks the good of the individual; the reciprocal model seeks a reciprocal relationship between group and individual for the good of both. The three models have grown and developed along with the rest of social work. The reciprocal model seems best to embody social work as it is practiced today and to lend itself best to a systems orientation, but there are still many agencies and many workers whose philosophy reflects both the social goals and the remedial models.

Group work techniques

It is important to recognize that differences in philosophy do not change the process of planned change. Whether dealing with groups, families, or individuals, the worker moves through the same stages. In working with groups, the worker may find that the group is already formed, and then move on to the first step in forming a relationship. This is particularly likely to be true when a worker takes over a group from another worker or begins work with a natural group. The film *Boy with a Knife,* starring a young Steve McQueen, depicts a young worker who hangs around a hot dog stand with a gang of boys until they learn—eventually—that he can be trusted.

The relationship established is more involved with a group, because it is not a one-to-one relationship, but involves worker-group member, as well as group members, with each other. Considerable study has been made of group dynamics. Cartwright and Zander point out that groups are "inevitable and ubiquitous," that they produce dependence, attraction, and acceptance, but that they also produce dissonances among members.[13] For the worker, these group properties mean that his or her knowledge, skills, and values must work together to seek out the aspects of the relationship that will be useful to each member as well as those that will be most useful to the group and to society as a whole. Establishing a group relationship is as important as—and even more dynamic than—establishing a relationship with an individual or a family. Working toward change also requires that the worker be clear as to what change is sought by the group, by individuals, and by the agency, and that he or she knows how to keep the group working on these goals.

Lawrence Shulman has made concrete suggestions for implementing the five central tasks. First of all, he suggests that there are two categories of techniques used by the worker in carrying out such tasks. Cognitive techniques involve *knowing;* transitive techniques involve *doing* to someone or something. Secondly, he lists cognitive techniques, as follows:

1. *Identifying the common ground*—The worker must *know,* in his own mind, what common ground exists between the client's or the group's perception of reality, and his or his agency's. In the above example of the elderly ladies' group, the worker accepted goal suggestions which had not originally been part of the plan. In a court-required group, the leader might have had to be much more directive, and much more firm in interpreting the goals of the group.

2. *Identifying obstacles*—The worker must *know,* in his own mind, what obstacles are real and which exist only in the perception of group members. Groups may suggest all kinds of reasons why they cannot meet regularly. The worker must be able to sort out the real from the unreal.

3. *Interpreting clues of verbal language*—Interpreting is a cognitive process which the leader uses for his own purpose. The term "old woman" used by one group member to another, may mean denigration, endearment, or merely that the members do not yet know each other's names. The leader must be able to interpret.

4. *Interpreting clues of non-verbal language*—Clues of non-verbal language are observable by a trained worker who works toward learning what clues mean. What, for example, does a group member mean when he turns his back on the person speaking? What does it mean when a member drums his fingers on the arm of his chair? What does a yawn mean?

5. *Identifying patterns of behavior*—Patterns of behavior can be identified only after some time. Individuals and groups eventually show some patterning which may be observed and categorized by the worker. Does one group member take umbrage at another member, regardless of the topic? Does one member always agree with the worker? Does another never agree with the worker?

6. *Contacting one's own feelings*—Contacting one's own feelings requires the worker to notice his own reactions in the same way that he has noted and observed those of the group members. When the client or group members use bad grammar, does the worker feel

uncomfortable? How does he or she feel when the client says "nigger" or "honky"?[14]

All of these techniques involve the worker's thoughts rather than his or her actions with the group member. They are more nearly related to the worker's values and knowledge than to skills. Just as the caseworker observes and interprets the nonverbal clues of clients, so the group worker observes and interprets nonverbal clues of each group member, and also of the group interaction. Cognition requires reflection and must precede the employment of transitive techniques.

Transitive techniques involve communications and problem-solving help. According to Shulman, communications include:

1. *Stepping up weak signal*—What is a signal? When a group member says "Yes, but . . . ," and lets his voice drop, the worker may say, "But what?"

2. *Stepping down strong signal*—When a group member shouts, "I hate you," to another group member, the worker may interpose with, "You sound pretty upset" or "What are you so mad about?" What might the worker say if the outburst is addressed to him or her?

3. *Redirecting transaction to actual intended recipient*—Frequently group members address the worker when the message is really intended for another member. "Jack always comes late" might get the response from the worker, "Why not tell Jack?"

4. *Reaching for facts*—Reaching for facts involves the worker in asking for factual rather than feeling material. "I can't stand the way my mother looks at me" might produce questions from the worker as to when, where, and on what occasions the looks occurred.

5. *Focused listening*—Focused listening filters out the extraneous material or cuts short lengthy descriptions. It may also concentrate on feelings rather than information. The mother who says "I slapped my baby three times last Thursday—or was it Tuesday" is not really concerned about which day of the week it was.

6. *Reaching for feelings*—Reaching for feelings applies to the same type of effort as the above example. The worker may say, "How did you feel after you had slapped your baby?"

7. *Waiting out feelings*—If the mother in the above example hesitates, the worker may wait till she can express her feelings in her own say, rather than prompt or suggest.

8. *Getting with the client's feelings*—The worker may tell the mother, "I can see that you felt pretty bad about what happened."

9. *Sharing your own feelings*—The worker may say to a disgruntled group member, "I have times when I don't feel like coming too," or even, "I would rather have stayed home today too."

10. *Seeking out empathic help*—The worker asks other members of the group to empathize and support the member who is having a hard time getting out his feelings. Or the worker may observe a member who looks sympathetic, and simply ask how he feels.[15]

All of these techniques involve speaking to and hearing out group members. Can you give examples of each of these techniques as you have observed or participated in groups? Skill is combined with knowledge and values in communication, and communication must precede problem-solving help. According to Shulman, "the activity taking place within the group may be viewed as an intricate process of problem-solving, with each member and the group as a whole continuously faced with a series of tasks. . . ." It is the difficulty encountered in problem-solving that calls for the help of a worker, whose task, separate and distinct from those of the members, is to serve as a catalyst and a resource for their problem-solving efforts. Schulman's techniques, which follow, are movements through which this help is offered.

1. *Providing working data*—The worker knows something that the group members do not. He has knowledge of resources, laws, or other factual data, which he shares with the group.

2. *Confronting with contradictory reality*—Reality may not always be comfortable or convenient to face. The group may prefer to fantasize about what might have been or what they would like. The worker must confront them with the real situation before they get too carried away.

3. *Pointing out obstacles*—The obstacles which the worker recognized to himself must be shared with the group so that they can work productively.

4. *Pointing out the common ground*—The common ground, previously identified by the worker to himself, must be pointed out to the group. "The agency agrees that you need to work toward a better recreational program for this group."

5. *Defining limits*—The worker explains that no one may leave the meeting room before 9:00 P.M., even though some groups have more flexible meeting times.

6. *Defining contract*—Once the group has come to some decisions

about what it will do, and what the worker will do, the worker lists the conditions.

7. *Partializing the problem*—Complex problems can usually be broken down into two or more parts. The worker must be able to take the lead in this breaking down.

8. *Making the problem the group's*—Problems of the individual remain his or hers unless the worker involves the rest of the group in the solving process.

9. *Waiting out the problem*—A group member may be unable to bring up what is bothering him but may talk of other things until he works up his courage.

10. *Offering alternatives*—A group member, or even the whole group, may need alternate suggestions when they reach what seems to them an impasse.

11. *Helping the client to see his problem in a new way*—Constant mulling over the problem may have made the group member or the group unable to see different aspects or different ways of looking at the problem.[16]

All of these techniques are closely related to cognition and communication. They are as useful with a single client as with a group, and they are part of the planned change process. Further, they are useful with both task and growth groups.

Task and growth groups

Some social workers, beginning with Gertrude Wilson, distinguish between groups whose main purpose is individual growth and those whose main purpose is the accomplishment of tasks. As in the three previously described models, the difference is one of philosophy rather than of technique.

The use of *growth groups* is a relatively recent development. In these groups, people who are not in need of therapy but think they could benefit from group experience meet with a leader who tries to help them increase their self-awareness, sensitivity to others, and general ability to see themselves through the eyes of others. The group is a useful tool for this kind of understanding, and while sensitivity groups have been abused and misused, there is clearly a great deal to be learned through them. That some people need them is fairly obvious, as is the need for trained professional leadership. The leader's knowledge of group tasks and techniques does not change in growth groups. The planned change process is again the method employed to move the group toward its goal.

Task groups are more nearly related to the practice of community work, which will be addressed in Chapter 8. Task groups are formed for the purpose of accomplishing a joint goal for a broad purpose. Examples of task groups are committees, clubs, boards of directors, and even governing bodies. The group is formed to accomplish something; when the task is completed the group may disperse or may move on to another task. Each individual has a role to play and a job to do. Nevertheless, the group leader, who may be called a *chair* or a *consultant*, must concentrate on the promotion of the planned change process and on an awareness of the various systems that are involved in the working of the group. He or she must keep in mind the central tasks and the cognitive transitive techniques used to keep the group at work on its task. The fact that the work has implications outside the individuals in the group does not mean that their individual behavior is unimportant or that their interaction with each other will not matter. Worthy causes will not make up for lack of cooperation on the part of participants. The group leader bears the responsibility for keeping the group at work on its task.

There is considerable similarity between growth groups and therapy groups, except that the leader's role is more reciprocal in the growth group—and the participants would hardly see themselves as in need of remedy. There is considerable similarity between task groups and social goals groups, except that the role of each member of the task group must be recognized as important to the group. And the group's ability to achieve its task is seen as important to the well-being of each member. Thus both growth and task groups seem to have reciprocal ends—to seek goals for individuals, for groups, and for the community at large.

Gerard Egan in his book *Face to Face* describes growth groups as *laboratory learning:*

> The participants come together in small, face-to-face groups in order to interact with and receive feedback from one another in ways that have been proved to develop a variety of human relations skills. Each member, by reflecting on his own behavior and by means of the feedback he

receives from the other members, has the opportunity to get a feeling for ("diagnose"), experiment with, and improve his interactional or human-relations style.[17]

Growth groups are also known as *sensitivity, encounter,* or *T* (training) groups. The two best known types of growth groups are encounter and T groups. While the two terms are used interchangeably, there is a difference. Encounter groups typically have no institutional backing, are unstructured, and are apt to be led by an untrained leader. They rely more on physical contact and nonverbal exercises, and emphasize an experience, rather than a change per se.

The T group started with Kurt Lewin, a German psychologist well known for his work in field theory, who emphasized feedback, interpersonal honesty, self-disclosure, unfreezing, and observant participation. The leader or trainer is concerned with the group's ability to learn and change, but sees them as functioning individuals who want to grow. The group members see the trainer as someone with more skills and knowledge, but not necessarily more prestige. They expect the leader to participate and they expect to model themselves on the leader. The T group nearly always has a predictable termination point, all members terminating at one time.

T groups are sometimes confused with psychotherapy groups or remedial groups, and there are commonalities between the two. Both groups seek to bring about hoped-for change. Both value self-disclosure on the part of the members. Both seek goals above and beyond individual goals, though these are more important in T groups. The differences within the group models may be greater than the differences between them. Some T groups appear to be quite therapeutic, while some therapy groups appear to be supportive and freeing rather than remedial. In general, though, psychotherapy groups are usually smaller, meet over a long period, and involve serious attention to the problems being considered. T groups may have twelve to sixteen members who may spend a great deal of time together for short periods, a weekend or a week. Generally, T groups enjoy their meetings and have fun. The psychotherapy leader is an expert and a professional, both in his or her own view and in the way the group views the leader. Psychotherapy group members are very aware of their own dysfunctioning and seek a leader who is omniscient. T group members, then, in general are well-functioning individuals who seek growth; therapy group members find it difficult to cope with everyday stresses and seek relief, first through their leader and eventually through the group.[18]

An outgrowth of T groups has been the evolution of self-help groups of various kinds. Their aim is to provide encounter and support for people sharing the same kinds of problems. Of these, perhaps Alcoholics Anonymous for alcoholics, Alanon for the families of alcoholics, and Parents Anonymous for abusing parents are among the best known. All make the assumption that the people best able to help with a problem are those whose own experience has been to know and deal with the problem. While social workers do not deny the effectiveness of this kind of group experience, they would suggest that following the theory to its rational conclusion would mean that no professional knowledge could be valid except personal experience. Since no one person can experience everything, social workers would be limited to their own experience. Even where the members believe experience to be all important, social workers frequently organize the groups or find and advertise the resources necessary to start a group. A knowledge of group and community theory is most helpful. While some T groups operate without leaders, social workers see themselves as participant leaders, perhaps models for other members of the group, but not teacher-experts ready with a diagnosis for each member. Since growth groups propose to enrich and expand individuals' self-awareness and sensitivity to others, they are somewhat like therapy groups, but since the members are healthy, functional people, therapy or remedy can hardly be their purpose. Take the following as an example.

The group was already assembled when the faculty member-leader arrived. Since the group was a requirement of the program, the leader asked how many of the members would have preferred not to be there. No one spoke up, but one member said, "If I felt that way, I wouldn't say so." The leader accepted this, and suggested that those who wanted to be there tell what they hoped would come from the group. Members said, "I'd like to know how I appear to others," and "I'd like to get to know the rest of the group really well," and "I hope we can be open and honest." The leader commended all these ideas and suggested that they start by introducing themselves and telling some bit of information that they did not usually include in an introduction. Do you think this was a T group or a therapy group? How do you think the members would relate to the leader in the other type group? Can you imagine an experience that you might have in either type group?

Still another important recent use of groups has been the group home. A recent article in *Social Casework* describes the use of group homes as a rejection of institutional care for children. Group homes have some of the advantages of foster home placement in that they approximate family life. But they are frequently more satisfactory for adolescents who have difficulty handling relationships with their own families. Further, group homes provide strong role models and a controlled peer group experience.

One variation of group homes sponsored by The Eckerd Foundation is the wilderness camping experience now being used by some states, notably Florida, North Carolina, and Vermont as part of their youth programs. Children aged nine through sixteen may be referred to the camps for periods of eighteen months through two years. Each group in the camp is led by two counselors who are strong role models, and each numbers ten campers of approximately the same age and ability. Mutual caring and responsibility are stressed as the groups perform regular camp chores like cooking, cleaning, building tents, and more adventuresome projects such as canoe or backpacking trips. The intent is to build a feeling of belonging, at the same time stressing each individual's responsibility. These programs require considerable parent participation. Each month and at all holidays, the children go home. Parents must visit camp regularly and consult with the staff. Experience in this kind of program provides a combination of all group models, both growth and task. It will be interesting to follow the experiment as more children from different backgrounds are involved.

In his article "Social Group Work: The Developmental Approach," in the *Encyclopedia of Social Work*, Emmanuel Tropp says:

> Society has moved into a period when people are seeking the human sustenance that has been lost in the course of technological development . . . and the generally increased complexity and depersonalization of societal structures. The search is for a new sense of community, with intimate and supportive human ties, giving larger meaning to individual lives through significant common purposes. To accomplish these ends, more and more people are finding for themselves their own mi-

crocosms of community. There are action groups to re-establish individual ability to make an impact on societal institutions; interpersonal
exploration groups in which individuals aim to find out who they really
are and how they appear to their fellow human beings; and groups to
pursue strongly held common interests, such as learning, experienc-
ing, or performing in the worlds of ideas and skills.[19]

Summary

Social group work, like social casework, seeks to promote better functioning of people through the planned change process. The three
models for social group work are the social goals model, the remedial
model, and the reciprocal model. The reciprocal model sees the
worker in the role of mediator between systems and adheres most
closely to a systems approach to social work. In any model, the
worker must bear in mind five central tasks and must use techniques
of cognition, communication, and problem solving. Task groups and
growth groups are reciprocal in their efforts on behalf of individual,
group, and community.

Notes

1. Michael Olmstead, *The Small Group* (New York: Random House, 1959), p. 21.

2. Olmstead, *The Small Group.*

3. Catherine Papell and Beulah Rothman, "Social Group Work Models: Possession and Heritage," *Journal of Education for Social Work,* Fall 1966, p. 66.

4. Papell and Rothman, "Social Group Work Models."

5. Arthur Blum, "The Social Group Work Method: One View," in *A Conceptual Framework for the Teaching of the Social Group Work Method in the Classroom* (New York: Council on Social Work Education, 1958), p. 12.

6. Gisela Konopka, *Social Groupwork: A Helping Process* (Englewood Cliffs, N.J.: Prentice-Hall, 1962), p. 111.

7. Papell and Rothman, "Social Group Work Models," p. 7.

8. Robert Vinter, *The Essential Components of Social Group Work Practice* (Ann Arbor, Mich.: University of Michigan School of Social Work, 1955), pp. 4, 6, 12.

9. Papell and Rothman, "Social Group Work Models."

10. William Schwartz, "The Social Worker in the Group," *Social Welfare Forum* (1961), p. 155.

11. Papell and Rothman, "Social Group Work Models," p. 10.

12. Schwartz, "The Social Worker," p. 157.

13. Dorwin Cartwright and Alvin Zander, *Group Dynamics: Research and Theory*, chapter 1 (New York: Row, Peterson, 1953).

14. Lawrence Shulman, *A Casebook of Social Work with Groups: The Mediating Model* (New York: Council on Social Work Education, 1968), p. 78.

15. Shulman, *A Casebook*, p. 77.

16. Shulman, *A Casebook*, p. 78.

17. Gerard Egan, *Face to Face* (Monterey, Calif.: Brooks/Cole Publishing, 1973), p. 6.

18. Irvin D. Yalom, *The Theory and Practice of Group Psychotherapy*, chapter 14 (New York: Basic Books, 1970). See also the third edition of this book, published in 1985.

19. Emmanuel Tropp, "Social Group Work: The Developmental Approach," in *Encyclopedia of Social Work*, vol. 2 (New York: National Association for Social Work, 1971), p. 1251.

PART THREE

Social service delivery in macrosystems

In the previous chapters we have referred to social agencies that provide the organization of social work. As we saw in Chapter 1 the agency has been sometimes public, sometimes private or voluntary. These two options will be examined. Education for social work is another indirect method of service delivery. So is community organization.

7

SOCIAL SERVICE ORGANIZATIONS

Most social workers live in a dichotomous world. They owe allegiance to their profession and clients, but also to their agencies. Traditionally, social services are delivered through agencies. Traditionally, agencies are either public or voluntary. In Chapter 3 we saw the various changes made in the Elizabethan poor laws and noted that these were the beginnings of public tax-supported responsibility for the needs. We saw also the growth of voluntarism in the United States, Canada, and Great Britain. It is clear that this supplements, but does not replace, public responsibility, though there have been periods when it was hoped that this could be true. When we have analyzed the two kinds of agencies we shall look at professionalism and ethics and try to make some generalizations.

Public agencies

Public agencies are defined by law—federal, state, or local—or a combination of two or three of these. Public agencies are supported by taxes and are therefore accountable financially and philosophically to the taxpayers. While the stereotype of a public agency is that of a large bureaucracy, some public agencies—for example, a county welfare agency in a small rural county—may be quite small. The director may be the caseworker, in charge of one or more payments workers.

Still, a bureaucracy may be defined as a formal organization characterized by clearly defined goals, specified rules, division of authority . . . with a recognizable social function to perform. (Perhaps size is part of the pejorative stereotype usually related to bureaucracies, like the tacit assumption that bureaucracy is connected with the public, rather than the private sector.)

It is true that public agencies must adhere strictly to their legal boundaries and that changes in policy or function cannot be made informally. They must also serve all clients who qualify. They may not refuse service to certain client systems. The usual services provided by public agencies are income maintenance, children's services, health and mental health services, and correctional programs. The intent is to help these client populations or to protect the rest of the population from these populations. Historically, we have seen that some populations, notably families and children, the aged, and the blind have received more special attention through the Social Security Act of 1935. More recently, the blind category has been expanded to include the disabled. All states must provide services to these categories, but the amount and quality of these services vary greatly among states and within states. Some states and some localities provide extensive services not only to these groups but also to others. In some states, services are very limited indeed. The important thing is that the public agencies are under direct mandate from the people, and that until that mandate is rescinded, agencies must continue to serve the population.

A recent example of a program in danger of being reduced is the food stamp program. Designed to help people with low incomes get more for their food dollars, the program has been accused of corruption in administration and use. A study by a graduate student showed considerable differences in perception by store managers and food stamp recipients as to what expenditures were made. The store manager saw expensive meats and luxury foods being purchased far more often than did the recipients themselves. Widely publicized abuse of the program has convinced taxpayers that this program is one that can justifiably be cut or dropped.

Since food stamps are provided through state, federal, and local auspices, the ramifications and complications of doing away with the program are great. In addition, many people receiving food stamps also receive many other services that will be affected. The food stamp question will be far reaching indeed. Currently, surplus foods are again being pushed as substitutes, despite their earlier lack of success.

Voluntary agencies

Voluntary or private agencies have a distinguished tradition of phil-anthropic social service. In England, the United States, and Canada, voluntary agencies have been developed by various groups, religious and ethnic. When special needs have been identified, special services have resulted. Some agencies have complemented services provided by public agencies, while others provide quite different services. Some public agencies originated as a result of voluntary agencies. Voluntary or private agencies have more discretion as to who shall be served and to what degree than do public agencies, whose services are prescribed by law. Private agencies must find funding through sources other than tax monies, though some tax money is theirs through purchase of service.

Historically, private agencies have been seen as being more auton-omous, more flexible, and more responsive to changing times and need than have public agencies. Their policies have been made by elected boards of directors, influential people who are concerned with and aware of specific problems in the community. Nonetheless, vol-untary agencies are not all, or even mostly, strictly local: Children's Home Society is a private, national agency with chapters in all states, and offices in many cities. Originally its purpose was to provide protection for unwed mothers and professional adoption service for would-be adoptive parents. In recent years, unwed mothers have be-come single parents. Not so many of them have sought protection, and fewer infants have been available for adoption. Children's Home Society, seeking a new charge, has turned its considerable profes-sional attention toward the problem of hard-to-place children, partic-ularly mentally and physically handicapped and older children. Local boards of directors have made decisions that seemed appropriate to their areas. Some boards have been more willing and able to change than others. But all have adjusted, have made compromises, without waiting for legal sanctions. Children's Home Society is still a re-spected private agency, performing needed social services. Other agencies have been less flexible and have found themselves without purpose or funding. Some of these have gone out of existence.

Voluntary agencies have usually been thought to be more profes-sional and more sensitive to changing need than have public agen-cies. The idea of private charity rather than tax-supported welfare has an undeniable appeal. So does the idea that certain groups can be served and others not served.

Nonetheless, with the passage of time, voluntary agencies have become less voluntary, while tax-supported agencies have become more so—in short, the line between the two has become blurred. The main difference has been funding. Tax monies have funded public agencies. But as more services are desired and supplied, public agencies frequently resort to purchase of service agreements. That is, public agencies make use of special services provided by private agencies, which the public agencies cannot or will not provide. For example, several states now purchase services from the Eckerd Foundation. As we saw in Chapter 6, the Eckerd Foundation provides "therapeutic wilderness camping" as a preventive measure for potential delinquents. Originally the private foundation operated two camps in central Florida. Referrals were accepted—or rejected—from teachers, social workers, judges, or families. The year-round camping experience for youngsters is supported by family counseling, regularly scheduled home visits, and conferences with the camp staff. A camper-staff ratio of about one to five is usual. Because the success rate is high, the state of Florida proposed purchase of service as part of its youth services. Other states followed. More camps have opened in Florida as well as in North Carolina and Vermont. States are thus able to avail themselves of a new and promising method of therapy without providing it through a public agency.

This has advantages and disadvantages. By purchase of service, the state is able to provide a service immediately for clients who might otherwise be consigned to a state training school. But the available service means that the state is less likely to make its own provisions more up-to-date. For the Eckerd Foundation, the added funds make expansion possible. The added state funds also mean prospective clients cannot be rejected without considerable evidence as to unsuitability. Nonetheless, purchase of service is clearly here to stay, and for many agencies it may make the difference between survival and extinction.

Voluntarism

Voluntary agencies depend for their ongoing services on professionals. Their very essence, however, is in the use they make of volunteers, particularly on their boards of directors. Boards are made up of volunteers, usually with some community status or some degree of expertise. On one board of directors for a local mental health association there were two physicians, one of whom was a psychiatrist, two social workers, a psychologist, three teachers, and four homemakers. Most of these people had the time, energy, and interest to spend some of each in promoting community mental health. Their interest would hopefully communicate itself to their friends and might recruit more members, some of whom would be potential board members. Volunteers are needed in many agencies for direct association with clients as well as for public relations, transportation, clerical work, and a variety of other activities. One of the most successful agencies in its use of volunteers is the American Red Cross. Recruitment, screening, and recognition of volunteers go on year-round, and volunteers provide many services that would otherwise be impossible.

Only within the last ten years have public agencies availed themselves of volunteer services. Perhaps because they have not been motivated, perhaps because they have not known how to proceed, perhaps because they have not had sufficient community status, public agencies are not accustomed to using volunteers. With the advent of the war on poverty, some innovative ideas were tried and some new programs promulgated. Among them was the use of volunteers and indigenous workers. In some cases the innovations worked better than in others. Substance abuse treatment centers could and did welcome and utilize former clients as volunteers. AFDC mothers could and did help each other with application forms and eligibility requirements. Furthermore, some volunteers became involved in community action programs designed to disturb the stability and tranquility of some agencies. Welcome or not, volunteers provided a new way of looking at public social services. In 1972, welfare recipients in Milwaukee wrote *Welfare Mothers Speak Out: We Ain't Gonna Shuffle Any More*. Their positions as volunteers in the Milwaukee County Welfare Rights Organization did not endear them to the public agency they complained about. Still, they performed a service for their fellow clients, and they were emphatically not paid staff.

Social work in nonsocial work settings

Before leaving the subject of social work in organizations we must note that many social workers do not work in either public or private social agencies. They work in hospitals, schools, clinics, and in private industry. They are medical social workers, school social workers, or industrial social workers. Thus their work may require that they work more closely with members of other professions than with other social workers.

For example, a school social worker typically works in a school setting. He or she may be responsible for one or more schools, acting as a liaison between student and teacher, student and principal, or student and family. The social worker may work much more closely with school personnel than with other social workers. His or her agency is the school, therefore professional identity must be guarded carefully against co-option or disappearance.

In the November 1980 issue of *Social Work,* Rosalie Bakalinsky wrote, "The value conflicts . . . must be boldly confronted and resolved, lest the profession be swept into a field of practice in which its basic mission and purpose can be negated."[1] Her thesis appears to be that social work cannot be practiced in an industrial setting because of differing values. Still, social workers have operated in a variety of secondary settings for a long time without being co-opted or overrun. If social workers can work in school, prison, and medical settings, surely they can work in industry. And they do.

Private practice

Social workers who practice privately are part of still another kind of organization. Private practitioners may set up practice on their own or, more often, in combination with other social workers. They may also practice with other professionals—psychologists, counselors, or psychiatrists. Historically, social work, unlike law or medicine, had its roots in agency practice. Only within the past twenty years have social workers—especially caseworkers—begun to regard private practice as an option. According to Sidney Lowenstein, several strains within social work have combined to produce more pressure toward private practice. These strains were:

> (1) The trend toward professionalization of social caseworkers; (2) The shift in the 1920s away from a purely sociological to a psychological and psychosocial approach to clients' problems; (3) . . . transfer of responsibility for income maintenance from voluntary and local agencies to

the national government through social security. . . ; (4) the policy of charging fees for services in voluntary and social work agencies, starting in the early 1940s; (5) diversification of settings with consequent expansion of relationships with members of other professions and the ensuing teamwork practice; (6) changes in status needs created by the movement of more men into a field in which women were almost the total work force; (7) mobility within social case work in order to "get ahead;" (8) increasing role and status stresses in career patterns which require changing from casework to teaching and administrative functions in order to achieve professional advancement; (9) divergence between competence in and opportunity to practice casework; (10) philosophical differences between the lay boards, which set agency policies, and employed professionals whose function it is to carry out the policies.[2]

Lowenstein's work is now over twenty years old and serves best as historical background, but the signs of stress that he perceived between the agency structure and some practitioners have persisted.

Some states, including California and, recently, Florida, have licensed clinical social workers. Many of these are in part-time or full-time private practice. In an article entitled "Agency versus Private Practice: Similarities and Differences," Herman Borenzweig revisited the questions of private practice. Among other findings, Borenzweig's study revealed that:

The poor, the old, the psychotic, children, young adults, and the aged tend to be served in agencies. As expected, the private practitioner tended to serve middle-class and upper-class neurotic individuals. The researchers were surprised to discover that more innovative modalities were used by workers in agency practice than by those in private practice. In private practice the one-to-one interview is the major practice modality. . . . The findings indicate that private practitioners and agency practitioners are different. Nevertheless, perhaps the differences between them are not as broad and significant as before. . . . The practice of social work in the private sector seems to be more acceptable to the body of professional social workers than it has been in the past and more similar to practice in other settings.[3]

Social work in organizations, as we have seen, may take a wide variety of forms. The traditional dichotomy has been voluntary-governmental, but the differences have become blurred, with voluntary agencies receiving grants from government and public agencies using volunteers. Social work is carried on in many secondary settings, including various types of industry, as well as schools, hospitals, and correctional and mental health institutions. Finally, some social workers organize their own practices and treat clients in a private setting.

Professionalism

Because social workers claim to help people help themselves and because, as we saw in Chapter 1, social workers subscribe to a set of values, considerable emphasis has been placed on professionalism. How can workers in such diverse settings as we have just described claim to have common roots?

Through the years, social work has vacillated between viewing itself as a people-changing profession and viewing itself as a profession for social reform.

Harry Specht in 1972 asserted that "the hallmark of a professional social worker is not his readiness to identify with a cause that supersedes fealty to any other. Rather, it is his desire and ability to proffer help to clients—rich or poor, black or white, oppressed, depressed, repressed, or whatever—within a framework of ethics and values."[4] Specht decried what he saw as "this attempt to borrow what appears to be the more potent knowledge and skills of professional lawyers and politicians."[5] He suggested that social work was headed away from professionalism and toward the status of a subprofession. He based his prediction partly on the moves toward advocacy and politicization and partly on the move by the National Association of Social Workers (NASW) to accept as members graduates of undergraduate social work programs.

Ten years later, Henry Miller, an equally eminent scholar, complained that social work students—and social work educators and practitioners—have abandoned the very people they have vowed to help. In a highly informal style (rarely seen in professional journals), Miller wrote, "The antiwelfare mob has gotten strong and powerful, and the *scary* thing is that they've co-opted us. They've been able to recruit the social workers to the cause of dismantling the welfare state."[6]

Quite clearly, social workers feel the need for different emphases at different times. The profession has vacillated between therapy and reform, between specialization and generic intervention, over the years.

The NASW is the professional organization that claims to sanction and regulate social workers in a variety of settings. Because of the tremendous variety of social work settings, the association's code of ethics, revised in 1980, is general and unexceptional. Nonetheless, the code can be seen to embody the accepted values espoused by all social workers. (See Appendix A.)

SOCIAL WORK EDUCATION

Education for the practice of social work has been traditionally graduate education. Since 1972, however, the NASW has been admitting to membership any graduate of a baccalaureate program approved by the Council on Social Work Education. The council is the accrediting body for schools of social work. In 1974, after considerable study and deliberation, the council began the practice of formally accrediting undergraduate programs. Not entirely by chance, the Department of Health, Education and Welfare began that year to fund undergraduate programs and students, sometimes at the expense of graduate programs and graduate students. The bases for accreditation were studied and tightened, as explained in a report by Betty Baer and Ron Fedrico: "The Undergraduate Social Work Curriculum Development Project was funded to the School of Social Work at West Virginia University for the purpose of improving and strengthening curricula at the undergraduate level. More specifically the goal became that of further explicating better educational objectives and the curriculum content essential to the achievement of those objectives. This report represents the results of efforts to achieve these goals.[7]

The report described the then current state of baccalaureate social work programs, analyzed the practice perspectives related to social work education, and made some recommendations about competences and essentials in undergraduate education. There are now over 300 undergraduate accredited social work programs in the United States—with more awaiting accreditation. Master's degree programs have also undergone growth, change, and general tightening of their requirements. Typically, master's programs provide opportunity for specialization built on a generic base. Not all professionals agree that the generic base can be acquired prior to graduate work, but nonetheless many master's programs now give advanced standing status to graduates in good standing in baccalaureate programs that are accredited. This means it is possible for these graduates to complete programs in less than the usual two academic years.

PH.D. PROGRAMS

Within the last ten years many schools have initiated doctoral programs. Today about a quarter of all graduate programs have doctoral programs offering study to about 800 students. This development indicates the profession's concern for professionalism and research. Most doctoral programs are research oriented but some emphasize teaching, advanced practice, or social policy analysis and development. The Council on Social Work Education advocates doctoral programs having goals and objectives separate from those of master's programs.

Most faculty positions in schools of social work now require or strongly recommend that candidates have a doctorate in social work or related field. But all faculty teaching practice courses must have a master's degree in social work.

Notes

1. Rosalie Bakalinsky, *Social Work* 25 (November 1980), pp. 471–75.

2. Sidney Lewenstein, *Private Practice in Social Casework* (New York: Columbia University Press, 1964).

3. Herman Borenzweig, "Agency vs. Private Practice: Similarities and Differences," *Social Work* (May 1981), p. 243.

4. Harry Specht, "The Deprofessionalization of Social Work," *Social Work* 17 (March 1972), p. 6.

5. Specht, "The Deprofessionalization of Social Work."

6. Henry Miller, "Dirty Sheets: A Multivariate Analysis," *Social Work* 26 (July 1981), p. 290.

7. Betty L. Baer and Ronald Fedrico, *Educating the Baccalaureate Social Worker: Report of the Undergraduate Social Work Curriculum Development Project* (Cambridge, Mass: Ballinger Publishing, 1978), p. 1.

8

SOCIAL WORK WITH COMMUNITIES

According to Roland Warren, "A community is that combination of units and systems which perform the major social functions having locality relevance." He further lists five major functions of community:

1. Production-distribution-consumption.
2. Socialization.
3. Social control.
4. Social participation.
5. Mutual support.[1]

All of these functions have locality relevance but are not necessarily confined to the locality. Also, all of these functions may be performed by some other types of social systems, groups, formal organizations, or whole societies.

According to Murray Ross in *Community Organization, Theory, Principles and Practice*, there are at least two kinds of communities.[2] First, a geographic community includes all the people living in a certain geographic area. An Indian village is clearly a community. The people living there are separate from the people in the next community, and separate from the people in the surrounding countryside. The same is true for all the other kinds of villages known to us throughout history. But as civilization becomes more complex, communities become larger and less clearly defined. A large town or big city may still be defined as a community in one sense, but it also contains a number of smaller communities. Political, economic, social, and religious communities are all separate and at the same time overlapping, even though the members of the community are all from the same geographic area.

Second, a community of interest is made up of people who share an interest or some interests, whether or not they ever see each other. Some examples are a political party, a church, or a professional organization. These people do not see each other regularly, but their concern for a particular subject allows their community.

Whether geographic or interest, the community is made up of people, individuals and groups. Thus community work for social workers can easily be seen as social work that involves larger numbers of people than either casework or group work. But a systems orientation shows clearly that mere numbers are only the beginning of the complexity. Every individual and every group relates differently to each other, to the idea of a problem, and to the idea of a worker who is expected to do something about the problem. All the knowledge, skills, and values of caseworkers and group workers are called into play in community work, as well as many more kinds of knowledge, many more skills, and many new values.

History of community work

Community work is both an outgrowth of other social work methods and a starting point for them. A very early nomadic tribe, believing in one deity, claimed to obey an injunction to "love thy neighbor as thy self." The Judeo-Christian tradition is built on the idea of all mankind as a community that takes into account the welfare of the whole world. Unfortunately, most people are not able to act according to this injunction. It is easier to recognize the connection between ourselves and those who are physically or mentally near to us. In medieval times, villagers gave allegiance to their masters, and masters needed their villages. With the growth of trade and craft, the population became more mobile, and fewer villagers lived and died in the same village, dependent on the same nobles. Some of these mobile citizens became old, ill, or for some reason, incompetent. Away from their own village they might well put undue strain on the resources of another community.

As mentioned in Chapter 3, the most famous, though not the first of a series of laws aimed at promoting local responsibility for the poor was enacted in England. The law 43 Elizabeth, enacted in 1601, came to be known as the Elizabethan poor law, and it was considered to be a model for its time, and for centuries later. Three basic principles were assumed: (1) the state is responsible for those unable to care for themselves; (2) the able poor and the unable poor must be differentially viewed and treated; (3) the unit of poor law relief is the parish.[3] The law provided for paupers in their own community, but by 1662, a more stringent Settlement Act was required because beggars still moved about. According to that act, each parish became responsible *only* for those who had legal residence within its bounds, which usually meant residence by birth. Furthermore, those without legal settlement had to be returned to their proper parish, and newcomers were required to post assurance that they would not become public charges.

This beginning of community responsibility worked toward the dilemma in community organization with which we must still deal: Should community intervention stress the delivery of services to individuals, as the poor law proposed, or should community intervention seek to modify those conditions that predispose people to functioning poorly? Should community work be concerned with treatment or reform? Should the view of social welfare be residual or institutional? Most authorities see that both points of view are needed. There is a need for social planning as well as for social development and social action.

Community work models

According to Jack Rothman, a leading writer in community work:

> There appears to be at least three important orientations to deliberate or purposive community change in contemporary American communities, both urban and rural, and overseas. We may best refer to them as approaches or models A, B, and C, although they can roughly be given the appellations respectively of locality development, social planning, and social action.[4]

The three models overlap, and according to Brager and Specht:

> Community organization is a method of intervention whereby individuals, groups, and organizations engage in planned action to influence

social problems. It is concerned with the enrichment, development and/or change of social institutions and involves two major related processes: planning (that is, identifying problem areas, diagnosing causes, and formulating solutions) and organizing (that is, developing the constituencies and devising the strategies necessary to effect action).[5]

Nevertheless, there is some advantage in discussing the three models as if they were separate and discrete.

MODEL A

Model A, locality development, is the particular interest of Murray Ross, who wrote *Community Organization, Theory, Principles, and Practice.* He traces the history of community organization from efforts at social reform and points to the alienation of people in today's industrial, urbanized society. He sees contemporary community organization as attempting to develop (1) meaningful functional communities as members of which individual citizens may have some sense of belonging and control over their environment, and (2) a new sense of neighborhood in the large metropolitan area through creation of citizens' councils and other forms of neighborhood organizations.[6] He uses the term *community development* to mean:

> the utilization under one single programme of approaches and techniques which rely upon local communities as units of action and which attempt to combine outside assistance with organized local self-determination and effort, and which correspondingly seek to stimulate local initiative and leadership as the primary instrument of change.[7]

This definition is taken from a UN document and related mainly to locality development in underdeveloped countries. However, the principles of locality development in the United States are the same. Community organization, according to Ross, is:

> The process by which a community identifies its needs or objectives, orders (or ranks), develops the confidence and will work at these needs or objectives, finds the resources (internal and/or external) to deal with these needs and objectives, takes action in respect to them, and in doing so extends and develops cooperative and collaborative attitudes and practices in the community. . . . The result of the community organization process, at any stage, is that the community should be better equipped than at some previous stage, or before the process began, to

identify and deal cooperatively and skillfully with its common problems.[8]

This model assumes that it is possible to bring about social change
through the participation of a large section of the community. If
something is wanted badly enough, so goes this theory, then all
members of the community will work together to achieve their goal.
While working together, they will heighten their sense of community
and take a greater interest in achieving their goal. This is an extension
of the social work principle of self-determination. Every community,
like every individual and every group, has a right to work toward its
own goals; and its work is more likely to be successful if more people
rather than fewer people are involved in planning and doing. This
model assumes that there is a very democratic makeup in the community. Community organization in early agencies, settlement house
programs, and Peace Corps projects followed the theory that everyone would work for the benefit of all. If differences existed, they
could be reconciled through rational, democratic discussion. Without
this effort at community development, agencies would have gone off
on their own bent, meeting needs as they saw them and overlooking
needs they did not see. The idea of cooperation and collaboration has
had tremendous effect on the efforts of social work reformers. Community councils, community chests, and councils of social agencies
have all tried to proceed in what they conceive to be a democratic way
to meet the needs of a community without duplication or neglect.
Sometimes, however, agency directors and board members have assumed their view of the community need was the only one. Their experience and knowledge presumably have made them better able to
make decisions about community needs than others in the community. Further, they are the members of the community whose power
makes their ideas work. They see the community as a homogeneous
entity rather than as a system made up of heterogeneous subsystems.

With this view of the community, what role does the locality devel-
oper/practitioner play? Usually, he or she is an enabler or mediator or
teacher. Since the community is a benign organization, the worker is
primarily concerned with coordinating, consulting, or lending a vision to the community leaders. Presumably, he or she works *with*, not
for, the community representatives. The worker views the whole
community as one. There is no suggestion that powerful figures in

the community may have different ends from the welfare of the community. It is conceivable, however, that these powerful people have more influence than some others. It is considered reasonable to cultivate them.

For example: The bimonthly meeting of the board of directors of the local mental health association was called to order by the chairman. His executive secretary, Ms. Poole, a social worker, sat at his right to take minutes. The main topic for discussion was the plan for a social club for returned mental patients. Ms. Poole had talked with each board member about the plan prior to the meeting. Some of the members who had said they would be at the meeting were not present. The Reverend Black, an old-time resident of Rivertown, seemed to be the outstanding opponent. He opened the discussion by saying flatly that the association could not afford to spend money on such an expensive project when no one knew if it would be used at all. He felt sure that his congregation would resent a special house for mental patients. Ms. Smith, the newest board member, said that, as a former mental patient, she knew the need for a social club in Rivertown was great. She felt that it was a good use for the group's money. The Reverend Black sniffed.

This is the kind of issue with which a locality developer deals. Hopefully, Ms. Poole has some information about the costs and use of social clubs in other communities. But the group must have some idea of the acceptability of such a project in this community. Is the Reverend Black a better judge of the community reaction or is Ms. Smith? Is it likely that the community, which funds the mental health association, will approve such a fund use? Ms. Poole will not have a vote on the question, but she will certainly have a voice in the discussion. Besides contributing data, she will be involved in lending a vision of the kind of community that supports a social club. She will also be a buffer between differing factions on the board. Because she believes that all the members have the best interests of the community in mind, she will smooth ruffled feelings and make sure that everyone's point of view is heard. Ms. Poole will be playing Shulman's mediating role. She will be recognizing the individual dignity of each member and will accept each. Her knowledge of this community, and of others, will come into play with her skill in bringing out all members' ideas, as will her values of democratic discussion and majority rule. She will work toward consensus among all the members, feeling that this group will be stronger and the community better if everyone is satisfied with the vote, however it turns out.

MODEL B

Model B, the social planning approach to community work, is oriented toward a problem-solving effort at social reform. Present-day community problems such as health, housing, employment, and recreation are seen by Roland Warren, one of the leading proponents of this approach, as being of such great import that they require high-level planning, both for prevention and treatment. Because of their size and complexity, these problems cannot wait for local democratic community processes for solution. Instead, professionally trained experts with a great deal of knowledge not available to the general public must study and work toward solving the problems. In their case book, *Community Organizers and Social Planners*, Joan Ecklein and Armand Lauffer describe the activities of social planners as follows:

> (1) fact finding and problem definition, (2) the building of communication or operating structures, (3) the selection and determination of social goals and policies in the design of action strategies, (4) some aspect of plan implementation, (5) the monitoring of change and assessment of feedback information. . . . Planners are not free agents. They are employed on a regular or consultation basis by organizations and groups. What they actually do, and the problems they attune themselves towards, [sic] are very much the functions of the auspices under which they work.[9]

The role of the worker, then, is that of expert. He or she must be expert in fact gathering, in analysis, and in knowing in depth what to do about problems, and must also have knowledge of the particular problem. Planning experts are not amateurs interested in enabling a community to solve problems in its own way. They use their knowledge at the request of powerful community persons, and are presumably hired by them. They are less concerned about conflict or consensus of interest, since these factual materials are regarded as incontestable. They see the client community as consumers of their knowledge and skills. Planners are less oriented to philosophies and practices of social work than their colleagues in community development, and more oriented toward research and evaluation, though they may have backgrounds in traditional social work.

For example: Jack Davis was a social worker who had been hired by the state for the express purpose of developing a program for the employment of developmentally disabled citizens. He had an advanced degree in special education for the developmentally disabled and he had worked with developmentally disabled children in a residential setting. His view of these people as citizens with rights and privileges was the result of considerable education and experience. The state legislature's bill calling for a program for the developmentally disabled seemed sensible and timely and necessary. Because he could cite national figures regarding the employability of such persons, Jack was able to convince some of the legislators that an employment program was in order. Because he knew and understood the general public's fear and misunderstanding of these people, he did not rely on a program develped by counties, to be financed by the state. Long conferences with local officials gave Jack a chance to hear their points of view, but he felt no need to give in or to settle for a compromise. He did behave courteously and diplomatically, but he left no doubt that his was the expertise, that he was the paid professional, and that the counties that qualified for state aid must abide by the guidelines laid down by the state.

What differences do you see between the approaches of Jack Davis and Ms. Poole? Do you think that the personality of each is the explanation? Do you think that Jack's method of operating shows that his training is superior to Ms. Poole's? Can you think of a situation in which the two might trade roles?

MODEL C

Model C, social action, illustrated by the work of Saul Anlinsky and his Industrial Areas foundation, regards process and planning as one device used by the establishment to forestall needed action.[10] To the social activists, the problem is always one of redistributing the power relationships in a community and, therefore, of providing goods or services to people in need. They do not see powerful figures as allies or as employers. Their view is that all problems are a direct result of power in the hands of the few to the detriment of the many, resulting in social inequality, social injustice, and social deprivation. They see all communities divided into two groups, the *haves* and the *have-nots*.

The task they see is to change these groups, at least in some areas. Their procedure is to crystallize issues, determine the target population, and take action designed to resolve the issues against the target population. The method they use is one of contest and conflict. Because they feel that they are destined to right a wrong, they see little room for consensus or collaboration or compromise. The practitioner's role is that of activist-advocate, one who sees injustice and allies himself with the oppressed rather than the oppressors. The activist-advocate is involved and partisan, not objective and remote. He is not concerned with democratic process, except in his own organization. He is not interested in long-term plans. His concern is with the oppressed segment of a community, and his efforts are directed at the overturn of the oppressors.

For example: Max Gold had had little experience with migrant workers before he came to work with the Miron County welfare department. As he listened to the requests for aid—most of which he could not fill—he became more and more angry at the county-state-federal system that provided elaborate regulations for giving no aid to migrants, who were mainly black, poor, and uneducated. Max asked Joe White, a migrant worker with whom he had become acquainted, if he thought the workers would come to a meeting. Max did not ask his supervisor or his county director. A rather small group showed up, mainly those who could be found that night by Joe. Max began by explaining that migrants are deprived of the rights that are theirs by law, because they had never questioned the regulations. Max wanted to make an example, to hire a lawyer, and make the county and state recognize the responsibility they had to migrants. Most of the people at the meeting shifted uneasily. No one said anything until one man asked timidly who would be the example. Max said Joe had volunteered. Someone else asked what would happen when the company found out. Max said the company probably would be upset. So what? Migrants were working for starvation wages anyway. A black man in the rear pointed out that they might well have no wages if the company were upset. Max asked how many had applied for welfare aid and been turned down. Several raised their hands. Max said they might as well save themselves the trouble of applying. Until they had a clear legal ruling, they would never get aid.

The next morning Max was called into the director's office and told that unless he put a stop to his agitating he would find himself out of a job. Max explained that the meeting had been a lost cause from the beginning. The workers did not want to establish their legal rights.

What is the difference between the approaches of Max and Jack Davis? Do you think Max's lack of knowledge is the difference between his reception and Jack's? How would Ms. Poole have proceeded in this situation? How would you have proceeded? Why? Do you think migrant workers are different from other community groups? Do you think a migrant community is different from other communities? Do you think Max would have had an easier time if he had been a black migrant worker's son?

Phases of planned change

In community work, as in the other methods of social work, change comes about at the instigation of someone. The community may feel the need—as in the state legislature that responded to constituents' dissatisfaction with current programs for the developmentally disabled. Or, it may be an agency worker like Max Gold who sees the injustice in the current welfare system and tries to do something about it. There are also cases where entire agencies perceive injustice and inequality, and some agencies have as their main purpose the attacking of current injustices. Or it may be an entirely different group —outside the community—that sees the need for change and initiates the process. The federal government frequently sets about changing local programs without being requested to do so by the locality.

In any case, once the initiation is under way, the problem must be studied, identified, and analyzed by someone. As in the case of the discussion of the mental health association earlier, the study may be partly of facts and figures, partly of feelings and biases and values. The community, like the individual, the family, or the group, must have its own individual analysis. Like the individual, the family, or the group, all communities have something in common, but all have their individual identities as well. These must be observed and evaluated, either formally or informally, by professionals or by members of the community.

Having sized up the situation, some plan must be developed,

some proposal for change. In locality development, the plan will include increased participation by members of the community, whatever the plan. In community planning, the problem will receive more attention than the process by which it is achieved, and in social action, the plan will include an effort to strip some power from the establishment and give it to some other group. Social activists feel, among other things, that power is a scarce commodity that is not shared, but held by a few. These few never give up their power willingly, so they must be relieved of it by pressure. Conflict is a necessary and inevitable attribute of all change, according to the activist.

Stabilization and generalization of the planned change process depends, as in casework and group work, on the success of the first part of the plan. In locality development, the process orientation posits that a successful experience for an involved community group will give them the courage and confidence to try again, either on another plan or on an extension of the current plan. Peace Corps workers who have been able to get the trust of their communities have found that building a successful road, or even a successful chicken coop, can give the community the kind of esprit de corps needed to attempt more difficult and involved projects. Neighborhood workers in large cities have found that picketing or writing a letter to a city official is sometimes encouraging enough to get the community started on another leg of a project. Conversely, the lack of success or lack of cooperation in the first step may well discourage any more efforts on the part of the community as a whole.

Community planners, less concerned with the process of change, feel that the merit of the actual problem-solving plan determines the success of further steps. The better the plan, they say, the more likely it is to work. However, they recognize that lobbying, educating, and publicizing contribute much to the success of excellent plans. A state's youth program that has been well thought-out and based on other experience and a thorough knowledge of the needs of this state may fail miserably simply because the legislature approves the program but fails to appropriate enough funds to make it work. Thus part of the plan must be to convince the legislature that the program must be adequately funded, even at the expense of some other worthwhile programs. Community planners, like social activists, sometimes recognize a scarcity of resources and the need to take resources from one group to give to another.

Social action gauges the success in stablizing and generalizing a plan of change by the amount of involvement, by the goodness of the plan, and by the degree to which the opposition has been forced to give up power. Civil rights groups, members of the women's movement, and labor unions recognize that *one* episode, *one* kind of strategy, will not change the balance of power in their favor. But they also recognize that a minor success in the beginning stage of their effort will provide encouragement for their own group as well as recognition by the general public and discouragement for their opponents. In systems terms, disequilibrium in any part of a system involves new inputs, processing, and feedback in the rest of the system. Social action sees the need for providing some of the disequilibrium, and then providing the means to prevent the new equilibrium from being the same as the old.

Finally, termination in community work may not be the same as is disengagement in work with individuals and groups. Some community work is ongoing; only the project changes. Civil rights leaders like Martin Luther King, Jr., did not see the end of community work for them and their cause. In King's case, his untimely assassination ended his part, but his program has been continued by other leaders. On the other hand, Peace Corps workers and other community workers in developing countries have aimed to get a program underway and then depart, hoping that the community will take responsibility from that time on. The planner also sees the end of one project and turns to another, which may have been engendered by the first. All of these examples assume that the worker makes the decision to terminate, but as in casework and group work, the choice may be out of the hands of the community worker. Sometimes the community terminates a program actively and decisively. They are unhappy with the project or with the worker, or they lose interest and motivation. Sometimes the community terminates by simply losing interest. Tasks are not done; meetings are unattended. One of the reasons for this type of termination comes in the early study and fact-finding stages. A community may decide to find out about the need for day care for children of working mothers in the community. A number of volunteers start conducting a survey. The more they survey, the more complex the problem becomes. After a few months of questionnaires and interviews, the volunteers decide passively that the job is too big and their facts and figures are not very helpful anyway. Bulky reports gather dust in the worker's office while the volunteers look around for a project that will get results quicker. Necessary as fact-finding is, it is all too easy to become so involved in it that it is never used; besides terminating a project too soon, enthusiastic volunteers are turned off without achieving the goal they have sought. What could have been a good experience in community service is a disappointment.

Termination of a project may also be the result of a force outside the community. The cutting off of federal funds is an example of sudden termination of many projects in the early 1970s. While most communities and most community workers will try to prevent the immediate effects of such cuts, they recognize that they are dependent on political and economic forces, not only for funds but for philosophic support as well. In the United States, enthusiasm for the Great Society, for example, was replaced by enthusiasm for law and order, and both were lost in the concern about inflation.

For whatever reason termination occurs, and whoever brings it about, an important aspect must be an evaluation of the project and its process. Community projects are particularly vulnerable to self-fulfilling prophecies. The supporters think the projects will succeed and opponents think they will fail. Without some built-in device for measuring, whose ideas will prevail? The commitment to evaluation requires that the project have carefully spelled-out goals and objectives in the beginning and that these be assessed at the end. If the goal is a new traffic light in a busy intersection, is the light installed? Is it promised? Has any progress been made? If so, what kinds of manipulations produced the change? Who was involved? What mistakes were made? If the goal is the passage of a legislative bill for licensing day care, did the bill pass? What held it up? Whose efforts were mainly successful? Whose efforts failed, and why?

Describe a community organization project in which you have been involved, and analyze its progress and process. Did you have an evaluative component? How could you have built one in? Successful termination assumes that evaluation has been completed. Even unsuccessful termination requires evaluation.

Brager and Specht have developed an outline for community organization process, which incorporates the development of an organization from small groups through institutional relations. The types of functions they describe are:

1. Socialization—the process of teaching individuals the values, expectations, and behaviors that the community considers important for them to learn. Usually we think of these in terms of children and their learning, but they are equally applicable when applied to adults in whom some change is desired. They key to socialization is the effort to change the individual members, rather than the society.

2. The formation of affective relationships, or primary groups. The function seeks to satisfy people's needs for social and emotional closeness with others. The key to primary groups is to bring about some change in the relationships between participants and to develop a sense of belonging.

3. The organization development function introduces people to others who share their personal, professional, political, or philosophical interests. The main task is to expand the constituency, broaden support, and develop new coalitions or organizations.

4. Institutional relations organizations seek to change organizations in the interests of the constituents of community efforts.[11]

All of these functions are a part of the planned change effort, and all seem to be required at some point for the development of a full-fledged institutional relations organization.

Similarities and differences

Like casework and group work models, the three models of community work are more alike than they are different. All three involve work with larger systems than casework, family work, or group work. All three use traditional social work knowledge, skills, and values, and all three require other additional knowledge, skills, and values. We have seen that each has different goals and involves different roles, as well as different techniques and different values.

Charles Grosser, in his book *New Directions in Community Organization*, suggests that, given an institutional orientation rather than the traditional residual view, clients and workers have equal, though different, roles. In many settings, including the Social Security Administration, clients contribute, receive benefits, and are sometimes also the dependents of a recipient. The workers are neither enablers nor advocates working on behalf of their clients. Instead, workers and clients work together to make policy. Both workers and clients suffer from dysfunctional social arrangements; both workers and clients need each other to cope with the complex social environment.[12]

Sometimes community work is broken down into neighborhood or grass roots community work and planning. While each of the three models may have some aspects of both, usually locality development and social action are seen to be more directly related to face-to-face work in neighborhood communities, while community planning is likely to be on a higher level. Still, it is accepted that all kinds of community work need planning in order to arrive at any kind of success. It is also accepted that both locality development and social action may be carried on at a high level. The idea of board membership at any level requires democratic process and diplomatic handling. As well as being a representative of the larger community, a board is a task group and, as we saw in the previous chapter, task groups have all the attributes of other groups.

Because professional social workers in casework, family work, and group work sometimes see community needs before others in the community, all social workers need to know something about community organizing and the process for intervention, development, and planning. Many new projects in women's issues, health programs, and child welfare have been initiated, developed, and carried on by social workers whose primary job was much more limited.

Social work administrators consistently carry out community planning, regarding this as a proper function of their jobs. While they do not devote all their time and energy to planning, they have a considerable stake in being on top of the kinds of activities that planners do.

All kinds of community workers must be aware of and understand the funding of their community, their project, and the funding of both larger and smaller groups with whom they may be connected. While this is true to some extent with caseworkers, family workers, and group workers, their familiarity with funding is not quite so vital as it is for workers concerned with planning, development, or social action. The former are not usually the people who make decisions about raising and spending funds. Community planners may have control of large sums for a project. On the other hand, locality developers may spend much of their time working out means for raising even enough funds to buy office stationery and to pay the telephone bill. Social action groups, such as the Farm Workers Union, must figure out the best way to accomplish a great deal with almost no funds.

Another unique contribution to community work is the extensive use of volunteers. Volunteers are used in casework, family work, and group work agencies, but not extensively and only in specific, limited jobs. In community work, volunteers are a vital part of any operation, from top-level planning to stuffing envelopes for sending mailings. Community work is built on and for volunteers. Locality development regards the involvement of all kinds of people as the first priority for success. Social action needs an actively participating group to counter established power. Board membership in planning agencies is frequently made up of volunteers whose expertise is related to the problem at hand.

An example of volunteers in community work is the Community Chest or Council, which seeks to coordinate fund raising, priorities, and planning for all the agencies in the community. Members of the board of directors are probably volunteers, powerful men from business or the professions, usually with a token homemaker representative. This board decides on the basis of agency presentation which money shall be given to whom and for what purpose. The board then sets a quota to be filled by various fund-raising teams, all volunteers. Publicity for the campaign is arranged through and by volunteers, many of them homemakers. In a large city, professional workers may coordinate all these activities, but in a smaller community only the director (assisted by a clerical staff) may be a professional. All other tasks may be done by volunteers.

Working with volunteers requires certain special kinds of knowledge and skills. Volunteers are not clients and they are not paid workers. The rewards that they can expect to receive from volunteer work are subjective and personal. Committed, dedicated volunteers are vital to community work, but one of the prime reasons for losing volunteers can be the lack of interest and concern on the part of the professional worker or workers. Since the 1960s, a new type of volunteer, the indigenous worker, has been sought by various agencies. Indigenous workers come from the client group and presumably can work in ways unknown to professionals, because the clients are more likely to trust their own neighbors. The concept is a good one, because indigenous workers are likely to have a commitment to the kind of work being done and because it is high time that clients were consulted about the kind and amount of service they want. Some projects require client representation on planning and policy boards in order to qualify for funds. Thus clients and policymakers become one and the same. To perform their best service, these policymakers must have the same status, the same respect, as any other policymakers. They may need more support from the professional workers because they recognize their lack of power and are not sure they will be heard.

For example: Silver City's Community Action Program was made up of "community leaders" such as real estate brokers, lawyers, a physician, and three businessmen. In order to qualify for federal funding, they had invited a construction worker to join their group. On the first meeting night, Mr. Smith, the construction worker, who was black, arrived first. He chatted with the social worker, who was the only paid professional on the project. As the other members arrived, the social worker introduced Mr. Smith, who was then ignored. During the discussion of housing problems, the social worker made a special point of asking for Mr. Smith's views and experience. Mr. Smith's technical knowledge of construction problems became clear, and the community leaders listened.

Do you think Mr. Smith should have been one of the original members of the CAP? Why do you think he was not? If you were Mr. Smith, would you have accepted the assignment? Why? What role do you see the social worker playing in this sketch? What other possible roles might the social worker play?

Summary

Community work, like casework, family work, and group work is concerned with people and with social systems. The social systems in a community are larger, but they are still made up of individuals, families, and groups. Communities may be geographic or interest, or both, and the social worker who works with communities needs to know about communities generally, and his or her particular community specifically. There are at least three conceptualizations of work with communities: locality development, social planning, and social action. While these overlap and are sometimes practiced together, each has its own theory, goals, roles, and techniques. Like models in casework, family work, and group work, all use social work knowledge, skills, and values, and all make use of the planned change process.

Notes

1. Roland Warren, *The Community in America*, 2nd ed. (Chicago: Rand McNally, 1972), pp. 9–10.

2. Murray Ross, *Community Organization: Theory, Principles and Practice*, 2nd ed. (New York: Harper & Row, 1967).

3. Arthur E. Fink, *The Field of Social Work*, 6th ed. (New York: Holt, Rinehart & Winston, 1974), p. 20.

4. Jack Rothman, "Three Models of Community Organization Practice," in *Social Work Practice 1968* (New York: Columbia University Press, 1968). Reprinted in *Strategies of Community Organization*, eds. Fred Cox et al. (Itasca, Ill: F. E. Peacock, Publishers, 1970), p. 21.

5. George Brager and Harry Specht, *Community Organizing* (New York: Columbia University Press, 1973), pp. 27–28.

6. Ross, *Community Organization*, p. 6.

7. Ross, *Community Organization*, p. 8.

8. Ross, *Community Organization*, pp. 40, 50.

9. Joan Ecklein and Armand Lauffer, *Community Organizers and Social Planners* (New York: John Wiley & Sons, 1972), p. 211.

10. Saul Alinsky, *Reveille for Radicals* (Chicago: University of Chicago Press, 1946).

11. Adapted from Brager and Specht, *Community Organizing*, pp. 69–76.

12. Charles Grosser, *New Directions in Community Organization* (New York: Praeger Publishers, 1973), pp. 13–14.

PART FOUR

Some special concerns

Social work has traditionally concerned it-self with special populations, with international linkages, and with trying to see future developments. All of these have both direct and indirect implications.

Part Four is designed to provide students with some beginning awareness of and concern for issues concerning the profession as a whole.

9

SOCIAL WORK WITH MINORITIES

In a sense, we are all members of a minority. Whether we are very rich or very poor, members of any racial group, young or old, we belong to a group less numerous than the sum of other groups. Even membership in any given religious denomination makes us members of a minority. If this is so, why are we as social workers so concerned about minorities? The answer is that some minorities are privileged—the very wealthy, the very powerful, the aristocracy. Other minorities are less privileged—the old, the black, the poor, Puerto Ricans, Native Americans, Chicanos, Cuban Americans, the physically handicapped, homosexuals, and children are just some of the groups whose minority is a disadvantage in relating to the rest of society. Throughout history, the powerful minorities have made decisions for the rest of the world.

Direct practice

The deprived groups are of particular concern to social work and social workers for two reasons. The first is that social workers, like the rest of the population, need to be aware of and tolerant of the differences between themselves and the minorities in question. The second is that, unlike the rest of the population, social workers need to be conscious of and sensitive to the kinds of problems these differences make for the minority group members. At the same time that they intervene to help with the solution to these problems, social workers must be conscious of their responsibility to maintain and preserve those differences that enrich and make meaningful the lives of their minority clients. "Starting where the client is" becomes again an important effort.

To get back to the first concern—what are some of the differences between discriminated-against minorities and the rest of the population? The National Association of Social Workers (NASW) code of ethics (see Appendix A) states:

> I will not discriminate because of race, color, religion, age, sex, or national ancestry, and in my job capacity will work to prevent and eliminate such discrimination in rendering service in work assignments and in employment practices.

Social workers are mainly members of a majority group—white, middle class, educated. Their perceptions of the differences between them and their minority clients may be confined to obvious physical differences. Yet, the obviousness becomes less so when the racial characteristics are compared with racial characteristics of members of the majority groups. For example, one characteristic of Orientals is slanted eyes. When a sample of Orientals is compared with a sample of Caucasians, we see that this characteristic is more prevalent among Caucasians and less prevalent among Orientals than popular perception would indicate. The same is true of skin color and other "obvious" characteristics. Many percpetions, then, turn out to be myths in the same way as the welfare myths noted earlier.

Try this questionnaire:

1. Homosexual adults pose a danger as teachers of children.
2. Black males usually expect to be taken care of by women.
3. The Cuban American family protects its daughters.
4. Native Americans usually like the carefree life of the reservation.
5. Lack of knowledge of English shows a preference for foreign traditions.
6. Black children receive the same social services as white children.
7. Mexican Americans have little anthropological history to cite.
8. More black than white prisoners are incarcerated.
9. The reason for the above is lack of intelligence.
10. Many blacks have a strong natural body odor.
11. Puerto Ricans come to New York to get high welfare payments.

12. Lesbians cannot be good mothers.
13. Middle-aged women are unstable.
14. Developmentally disabled adolescents have highly sexual natures.
15. A history of mental illness precludes participation in stressful occupations.

These are just a few ideas commonly held by people, including social workers. Perhaps you can think of others, which, of course, you do not hold but others might.

It is evident that our knowledge and values about groups outside our own experience need constant scrutiny and change. What, then, as a profession have we done about this? What are we doing? What can we do?

Billingsley and Giovannini have written a book on black child welfare called *Children of the Storm*. They state:

> From the beginning of United States history, as we have seen, black children have been at least partially excluded from welfare services. . . . Five major sources of aid to children and families emerged among black people during the late nineteenth century; the black churches, black schools and colleges, black lodges, black women's clubs, and black philosophy.[1]

The writers accused U.S. child welfare services of two evidences of racism:

1. Failure to develop services for children in their own homes, which was particularly disadvantageous for black children.
2. Failure to include black children in existing services.[2]

Yet, when these failures were cited, U.S. social work and social workers were committed to the ideal of equal distribution of services for all, "regardless of race, color, religion, age, sex, or national ancestry."

Despite the code of ethics, the profession has been guilty of discrimination, according to Billingsley and Giovannini. Since the actions of the profession are a result of individual perception and action, perhaps each individual should consider what he or she can and should do. First, we need to raise our own consciousness. We must examine our attitudes and perceptions. We must also be aware of our "knowledge" and its sources. For example, most Americans' information about Native Americans and Mexican Americans is gained through reading history books researched by American scholars whose ultimate sources are American and Spanish—not Native American or Mexican American. Only recently have some popular books appeared to give some perceptions of another view. *Bury My Heart at Wounded Knee* by Dee Alexander Brown describes an American attack on Native Americans.[3] *Roots* by Alex Haley describes the evolution of one black family beginning before the family was brought to the United States.[4] Both of these books were sympathetic to the minority, rather than to their majority oppressors. They are exceptions. But if our history reading had contained more of this view, we *might* have different perceptions of the people involved.

U.S. history is full of instances in which various groups were oppressed—Catholics, Jews, Irish, and Italians have all had their turns at being used and abused by the larger society. Most survived. So why are we concerned about the discomfort of current minority groups? Social workers, at least, feel that such oppression is human but inhumane. A laissez-faire policy is not congruent with social work values.

In *Social Work: A Profession of Many Faces,* Morales and Sheafor define social work skill as:

> the social worker's capacity to set in motion, in a relationship with the client (individual, group or community), guided psycho-social interventive processes of change based on social work values and knowledge in a specific situation relevant to the client. The change that begins to occur as the result of this skilled intervention is effected with the greatest degree of consideration for and use of the strengths and capacity of the client . . . the social work method is the responsible, conscious, skilled disciplined use of self in a relationship with an individual or group. It includes systematic observation and assessment of the client and formulation of an appropriate plan of action.[5]

The key words seem to be "consideration for and use of the strengths and capacity of the client." It is hard to consider and use strengths and capacity if we do not know what they are. This is where social workers differ from the rest of society. They expect and find strengths and capacities in clients who appear to have only problems. One obvious way for social workers to discover these strengths and capacities is to learn the clients' language. Schools of social work rarely require that students study a foreign language, but there is no doubt that even a little knowledge of Spanish would be a helpful skill in working with many Spanish-speaking minorities. Expressing one's intimate and stressful feelings in a foreign language is a difficult task, as anyone who has tried it knows. But more than communication is involved. A worker who will at least attempt to speak to a client in his or her own language indicates a commitment, an interest, an involvement.

Communication in English is hard enough with white, educated, middle-class people. Communicating with people whose lifestyle is different, whose customs are different, who think differently, is difficult. It is even more difficult if we rely on our usual patterns of thought and action.

For example: An attractive, well-dressed woman in her mid-twenties appeared for an appointment at a traditional family service agency. Her stated reason for coming was that she had a "personal problem." The caseworker, a middle-aged male with many years' experience with family counseling, tried to put his client at ease by saying that many young couples had problems at first, and that it usually helped to talk them out. He suggested she tell her story in her own way. She did. Her description of a stormy relationship full of domestic crises and sexual jealousy was nothing new to the worker. He said little, nodded sympathetically, and when at last she paused for breath, asked how long she had been married. Calmly, she explained that her partner was another woman and that they had not thought of marriage. The worker, embarrassed and confused, asked if either of the women had had psychiatric help. Rather tartly, the young woman said there was nothing wrong with their psyches—it was the relationship they were concerned about.

The worker had read articles about gay rights and had seen accounts of requests by homosexuals to stay in the military service, keep their jobs, and even their children. Still, he was caught off guard by the actual request for help from an avowed homosexual. To his own embarrassment, he returned to an earlier pattern. His traditional view had accepted the idea that homosexuals must be mentally or emotionally ill. The experts who described homosexuality depended on case studies of troubled people—therefore all homosexuals must be sick. The caseworker skilled in marriage counseling was not at a loss to define a plan. He simply made a mistaken assessment. In this case, he was able to recover his aplomb and continue to learn more about the strengths and capacities of the two people involved.

Successive appointments were made with both partners. The relationship, which had many strengths, was improved by more open communication, and the partners felt they were better off than before.

One advantage the male caseworker had was his background of recent information about sexual preference. He knew that the American Psychiatric Association had removed homosexuality from its list of illnesses. He knew and approved the action of many states in supporting civil rights for homosexual citizens. He knew and sympathized with the concerted action of gay groups in Miami where Anita Bryant mounted her Save Our Children campaign. The worker was not concerned about the threat to children. He was aware that more children are propositioned by members of the opposite than of the same sex. Because he had this background of knowledge, he was able to recognize his own bias and to exercise his skill in spite of it. Not all workers would do so well.

Marva White was a young, attractive, and enthusiastic black woman. A recent graduate of a master's program in social work, she had accepted a position with the Veterans Administration Hospital social service. One of her first clients was Mr. Ames, a middle-aged white man who was being released after treatment for ulcers. Mr. Ames confessed that he was very worried about finding a job. He was divorced, paid heavy child support, and the doctor had told him he could not do construction work—his previous job. He wondered if his 40 percent disability would convince the court that he could no longer make the payments. Marva was disgusted and showed it. Here was a white male, one of the privileged class, trying to get out of his obligations, and expecting her to help him. Marva thought of all the black women she knew whose husbands had deserted, leaving wives and children with little choice but welfare. She thought of all the families headed by women because their husbands had no jobs and no chance of getting jobs. Without knowing any more about Mr. Ames than his brief explanation, she categorized him as a shiftless, whining crybaby without enough gumption to get out and find a job. In her conference with her supervisor, Marva so described him. Her supervisor, a black woman, asked some pertinent questions about Mr. Ames's personal life, job history, and physical condition. Marva did not know the answers and admitted thoughtfully that her conclusions about Mr. Ames were based on her preconceptions of white men as a group rather than on her knowledge of Mr. Ames as a person with strengths and capabilities. Fortunately, Marva was able to see and understand her own attitudes and feelings. If it was too late to be much help to Mr. Ames, perhaps she would do better with the next client. Marva's supervisor helped Marva to see that black workers have problems relating to white clients just as white workers do to black clients.

Before her marriage, Marie Roberts had been Mary Redfern. Brought up on an Indian Reservation in northern Minnesota, she had excelled in school, gone to high school in nearby Hibbing, and worked her way through the University of Minnesota. She was proud of her achievement and hoped to work with poor adolescents in Minneapolis. Her first job was with a neighborhood information center in south Minneapolis. Many of the clients were Native American, some were black, some were Asian American. Most were white, with a variety of ethnic backgrounds. Marie related well with adolescents and soon had a reputation for dealing well with "difficult cases." So she was surprised when one day her supervisor suggested that she spend more time getting acquainted with the parents of her clients. Marie pointed out that the reason she related so well with adolescents was that she understood their problems with their parents. Native American parents expected their children to deal with problems within the family. So did Asian American parents. Their children did not. The supervisor asked if she were not reliving her own adolescence, refighting the same battles but with different characters. Hurt and angry, Marie reminded the supervisor of how well she had done in spite of overwhelming odds. The supervisor agreed that Marie's experience had been invaluable. But it was a personal experience, not one that could be repeated for every client, every adolescent client, or even every Native American client. Further Marie still had many problems to work out in relating to her parents, extended family, in-laws, and others. To think she had the answer to adolescent revolt would be presumptuous. All this was discussed with much participation by Marie, who admitted that a peer relationship that she was offering to adolescents filled her needs first and theirs second.

Encounter with Saul Alinsky is a film distributed by the National Film Board of Canada in 1967 that portrays the late Saul Alinsky discussing strategy with a group of young male Roma Indians in Canada. The young men are complaining about the treatment of Indians by the

Canadian government. Alinsky suggests direct confrontation and an effort to embarrass the government. Although they are clearly impressed by Alinsky, the young men resist his ideas, suggesting that their culture has something to offer. Alinsky disagrees vehemently. He says their culture has been kept down because the Indians were unwilling to fight back. Unfortunately, we are left with no answers, but with an impression of Alinsky's abrasive style. Few social workers would regard this as a model for dealing with minority problems.

Minorities and indirect practice

If human service organizations provide challenges for Caucasian workers and administrators, the experience of minority members must be even more fraught with stress and tension. Despite statements of equal opportunity at all levels of government and in much of the private sector, evidence is available to show that discrimination does exist. The United States Office of Personnel Management provides a brochure describing its conditions for employment: "All applicants for Federal employment receive consideration without regard to race, religion, color, national origin, sex, political affiliation, age (with authorized exceptions), handicapping condition, or any other non-merit factor."[6]

Since 1972 such statements have been required, not only by governmental agencies, but also by those agencies that receive some governmental funding. Such statements have not provided equal opportunities for all, but they have indicated a sensitivity to the need to go beyond offering equal opportunity at the starting line. "Freedom is not enough," Lyndon Johnson said. "You do not wipe out scars of centuries by saying now you're free to go where you want and do as you desire. You do not take a person who for years has been troubled by chains and liberate him, bringing him up to the starting line of a race and then say, 'You're free to compete,' and justly believe that you have been completely fair."[7]

In the *New York Times*, March 2, 1986, Kenneth Noble cited the various responses by companies who do business with the federal government, and who therefore must comply with affirmative action regulations. Large companies, heard through the National Association of Manufacturers, support the use of goals and say they have been effective in bringing women and minorities into the workplace at all levels. The Chamber of Commerce, representing smaller employees, claims the government goals are too specific and proof of effort is too demanding. This is the argument made by some Reagan administration officials. Still, there seems little doubt that more progress has been made since federal favors made affirmative action profitable than in the many years when "fair employment practices" were given lip service but with no requirements.

Like most social problems, discrimination in employment is only a part of an interwoven pattern of discrimination in housing, education, income, services, and everything else that goes into the making of minorities. Nevertheless, it seemed for a decade that some progress might be made toward decreasing discrimination. When the Reagan administration limited the extent of affirmative action requirements in 1981, this progress seemed destined to halt or perhaps even to be reversed. Even in cases where minorities are employed, their promotion and salary increases tend to lag behind those of white middle-class males. Even in cases where minorities are definitely qualified, their work may be more critically assessed than that of other workers.

Ms. Wood had worked in the public assistance office of Atlanta for thirty years. Without benefit of graduate education she had worked her way to the position of casework supervisor. She prided herself on being a fair, efficient, middle management person, able to juggle the needs of her work and the demands of administration. Her workers and superiors concurred. One day a young black graduate of Atlanta University School of Social Work, Mr. Trent, was assigned to Ms. Woods' department. His background in research and administration was impressive. His field experience directly with welfare clients was meager. Ms. Wood assigned him a minimum caseload and assured him she would be available for consultation. Unfortunately, with the annual report due next month, Ms. Wood took several days of annual leave, and a backlog of work built up. Mr. Trent found himself needing help and turned to other workers not much more experienced than he. Ms. Wood suggested he not do this. The sudden departure of one worker left an uncovered caseload. Mr. Trent received ten more cases, some very demanding. At the end of the month, his work was not up-to-date, two of his clients had called to complain, and he was ready to quit. In her final conference with him, Ms. Wood explained kindly that social work is demanding and stressful, not for the fainthearted or the theorist. Perhaps Mr. Trent would prefer to be in another department? Perhaps so, but there is more than one way to indicate disapproval of one who is black, male, and educated. Ms. Wood was a very experienced administrator.

One minority, really a majority of the general population, has made considerable impact on employment, especially in human services in the past ten years. Women have entered employment in increasing numbers during the 1960s and 1970s. Social work has been known as a women's profession, despite the fact that men have traditionally held administrative positions. Julia Rausch says, "It has been well documented that female social workers are tracked into casework positions, receive lower salaries than their male colleagues, and are less likely to advance professionally. Other frequently discussed dilemmas confronting female professionals include dilution of their commitment to a career by role conflict, interruption of their careers, multiple family responsibilities, subordination of married women's careers to that of their husbands, and even the 'motive to fail.'"[8]

Racism and institutional racism

Racism has been defined in many ways by many authors. No one definition covers the topic. Brieland, Costin and Atherton say: "Racism comes from a recognition of differences, the placing of a negative value on the differences leading to inferiority, superiority, and the generalization of the negative characteristics to all people in the group. Skin color has already been identified as the most evident basis for racism."[9]

A direct result of this way of thinking is *institutional racism*. Institutionalization involves formalizing values to form policies and laws. Sometimes refusal to enforce laws and policies results from institutional racism. Federal civil rights acts, and affirmative action policies can be, and are, undermined by efforts to dilute their impact. These efforts may be made by individuals acting as representatives of employing agencies, or simply acting on their values as they see them. For the most part racist values are not regarded as such by the people holding such values. Even less is institutional racism recognized as such.

At a conference on institutional racism, a white participant was bewildered and hurt when accused of racism by a black participant whom he had referred to as a "good boy." The black participant was forty-five years old.

Feminization of poverty

The feminization of poverty has been in process for a number of years, but in the 1980s it has come into full flower. Women (or, less frequently, men) with children and no income are entitled to welfare payments in the form of Aid to Families of Dependent Children. They may also receive food stamps, medicaid, and subsidized housing. They may not receive subsidized day care. If they work, their grants are reduced by the amount they earn. In 1968, the poorest one fifth of all families had, on the average, 91 percent of the income they needed for basic needs. In 1983, they had 60 percent of income needed. Most children in families headed by women are poor. Fifty-one percent of all poor children live in families headed by women. For children in families headed by women under thirty who did not complete high school the poverty rate is over 90 percent.

These statistics, compiled from the Congressional Research Report of 1985, describe an increasingly dreary prognosis for a growing segment of the population. Single mothers, whether never married or formerly married, are less able economically to provide for their children than are two-parent families or one-parent families headed by a father.

The *New York Times,* May 17, 1985, reported that more than 25 percent of all families with children in the United States have only one parent present, up from 21.5 percent in 1980 and 12.9 percent in 1970.

Mothers continue to predominate in caring for children in one-parent households—89.1 percent, as compared with 10.9 percent headed by fathers.

Even among families above the poverty line, the family income of female-headed families is lower than that of male-headed families. Divorce arrangements generally assure the increase by 73 percent in income of the husband-father. The wife/mother and children experience a decrease of about 40 percent.

Figures for black families show the same trends but with even greater numbers of poverty families headed by women.

Summary

Working with minorities poses special problems for social workers because they must not only recognize and tolerate the perceived differences but they must also appreciate the problems caused by the differences, and work to preserve the richness these differences bring to the culture. These two requirements demand that social workers appraise continuously their own knowledge and attitudes and work continuously to improve their skills in relating, assessing, planning, and executing with their clients, always taking into consideration the clients' strengths and capabilities.

Notes

1. Andrew Billingsley and Jeanne Giovannini, *Children of the Storm* (New York: Harcourt Brace Jovanovich, 1972), p. 45.

2. Billingsley and Giovannini, *Children of the Storm*, p. 101.

3. Dee Alexander Brown, *Bury My Heart at Wounded Knee* (New York: Holt, Rinehart & Winston, 1970).

4. Alex Haley, *Roots* (Garden City, N.Y.: Doubleday, 1976).

5. Armando Morales and Bradford Sheafor, *Social Work: A Profession of Many Faces*, 4th ed. (Boston: Allyn & Bacon, 1986), p. 228.

6. U.S. Government Publication (Washington, D.C.: GPO, 1979), p. 2.

7. Lyndon Johnson, "The Rights Revolution," *The Congressional Quarterly*, 1978, p. 159.

8. Julia Rausch, "Gender as a Factor in Practice," in *Social Work: A Profession of Many Faces*, eds., Armando Morales and Bradford Sheafer (Boston: Allyn & Bacon, 1986), p. 344.

9. Donald Brieland, Costin & Atherton, *Contemporary Social Work*, 3rd ed. (New York: McGraw-Hill, 1985), p. 206.

10

INTERNATIONAL SOCIAL WORK

The foremost international agency is the United Nations, with its research and information programs. Unfortunately, funding does not keep pace with requests for service. Still, every developing country has established a central ministry for provisions of social services. Social services, of course, mean different things to different nations. In many of the newer nations, education and health services at a very rudimentary level are only in the beginning stages. According to the *Encyclopedia of Social Work*, rural areas are less likely to be serviced than urban areas, but efforts in rural areas show the most marked development.

Such problem areas as population growth and housing have been focused on by the United Nations and received worldwide attention. Between 1960 and 1975 world population increased by 33 percent. Developing and developed nations alike have sought help with family planning programs, food supply, housing, and health services. Clearly, increased attention to social services is a mark of development, and another evidence that the interdependence of social systems is very real.

To Americans, the most tangible evidence of international social welfare is the presence of people from other countries on exchange programs. These may be officials, educators, legislators, practitioners, or volunteers. What they have in common is an interest in and concern for welfare programs.

So much of U.S. social work education is based on American experience and American literature that American students sometimes think that they are models for the rest of the world—or at least *a* model. This is not true.

In their book *Social Services in International Perspective*, Alfred Kahn and Sheila Kammerman discuss "the emerging personal services" as the prerogative of every industrial urban society. "Indeed," they say, "one could with some basis even argue the hypothesis that economic development and industrialization are more important determinants of social welfare focus and solutions than is political or economic ideology."[1]

Social work all over the world is concerned with personal service and service delivery, but the more sophisticated the country, the more emphasis is placed on preventive and support services. Kahn and Kammerman list the personal services as consisting of the following tasks:

1. Contributing to socialization and development; that is, offering daily living and growth supports for ordinary, average people (not just problem groups), a role shared with other nonmarket services but involving unique programs.
2. Disseminating information about, and facilitating access to, services and entitlements anywhere in the social sector.
3. Assuring for the frail aged, the handicapped, the retarded and the incapacitated a basic level of social care and aid necessary to support functioning in the community or in substitute living arrangements.
4. Arranging substitute home or residential care or creating new, permanent family relationships for children whose parents are not able to fulfill their roles.
5. Providing help, counseling and guidance which will assist individuals and families facing problems, crises, or pathology to reestablish functional capacity and overcome their difficulties.
6. Supporting mutual aid, self-help, and activities aimed at prevention, overcoming problems in community living, advocating changes in policies and programs, and service planning.
7. Integrating the variety of appropriate programs of services as they impact upon individuals and families, to assure coordination for maximum effect.
8. Controlling or supervising deviant individuals who may harm themselves or others, or who are under hazard, while offering care or opportunity for assistance, guidance, growth, or change.[2]

All of these social services are seen as appropriate functions of government by some countries, but not by all. In an article on intercultural aspects of social work, the late Eileen Younghusband of Great Britain has described similarities and differences in social work educators' perceptions of social work values, functions, and methods. "The Asians," she writes, "were much less troubled about the imposition of values than the Westerners and said that if social work values . . . are good values, then it is a desirable social work function to act as a change agent in the spread of these values. In any event, historical evolution everywhere is producing a convergence of values."[3]

Historically, as we saw in Chapter 3, most of the U.S. welfare traditions came from Britain. In the late nineteenth century and early twentieth centuries, Britain and most of Western Europe turned to social reform while U.S. social work turned to problems of individual adjustment. For a number of reasons, the discovery of Freudian psychology, the Puritan work ethic, relatively little poverty, and nonwelfare-oriented government, the United States has been rather slow to see social reform as a solution to social problems. Even when some reforms have been enacted, they have been spotty, uneven, and always much maligned. No one, for example, thinks of the United States as a welfare state, except in the most pejorative sense. Even though schools, highways, post offices, and veterans' benefits are paid for by the taxpayers for the public's welfare, we do not see these as functions of the welfare state. Rather, the United States reluctantly makes minimal and inadequate efforts to meet immediate and pressing needs of some citizens, and then wonders if we have gone too far with welfare. Are we in danger of becoming socialist?

European countries have had the advantage of living close to socialism, even of having direct connections with communism. Yet many European countries are at least as capitalistic as the United States, with more or less resources and wealth, and have chosen to deal with problems of social welfare differently.

Three examples might be Canada, Great Britain, and Switzerland. All are mixed capitalist-socialist countries. Canada, larger than the United States but with a smaller population, has similar but not the same problems as its southern neighbor. Great Britain, with a history of great colonial power and wealth, is now reduced to an island that does not and cannot produce enough to meet its own needs. Switzerland had been historically small, poor, and constantly threatened by aggressive European neighbors. Today it is one of the world's wealthiest countries, stridently capitalistic, but providing for many welfare needs of its citizens.

Canada

With 24 million inhabitants, Canada has roughly one tenth the population of the United States with a very similar number of square miles. Both are three-tiered countries—that is, political power is distributed among federal, state/provincial, and local governments. Canada is a liberal democracy under a parliamentary system. It is characterized by the cultural-language split between the English and French populations. While the former is the majority, demands by the latter have dominated Canadian politics and limited federal consolidation. Most social services are locally operated, though this varies by province.

As in most three-tiered governmental systems, the breadth and depth of social service coverage varies greatly from province to province and from locality to locality. In child welfare services of all kinds, in services for the elderly, and in general personal social services, the Canadian national government provides 50 percent matching grants to provinces that in turn provide funds to localities. A taxable family allowance is one major supplement provided in Canada but not in the United States. Another supplement is a provincially administered hospitalization and health program supervised by the Federal Department of National Health and Welfare. Like the United States, Great Britain, and Switzerland, voluntary services are an important part of the welfare program, and heavily subsidized by the federal government.

Great Britain

Next, let us consider Great Britain. It has been a model for the United States since the latter was thirteen colonies. Beginning with the poor laws and their admission of local responsibility, the British have recognized and perceived an ongoing need for such responsibility. At first, the group needing support was thought to be a small temporary portion of the population whose demands required attention but whose greater need was character reform. As time went by, more and more people began to recognize that individual needs required institutional rather than character reform. Old people, disabled people, and children all needed some kind of provision other than on an individual basis. In the parish of St. Botolph's, Aldgate, just outside the city of London, records show that a man who had lost a leg applied to the parish wardens for a license to beg. After some consideration, the wardens gave him the license, believing they had done their Christian duty. Some years later, a woman whose husband had left her applied to the wardens for support. Again the group agreed that this was a worthy cause. This time each parishioner was charged an amount judged to be within his ability to pay. Presumably, each time the wardens levied a tax the parishioners paid up. Presumably, the parishioners approved the tax. At least they knew where it was going and for what purpose. At least they accepted their responsibility for parishioners less fortunate than they.

The almshouse, relief to individuals in their homes, and eventually institutional care for particular groups were tried with greater or less success in Britain, depending on the era and the perception of the problem. By the latter part of the nineteenth century, when the Industrial Revolution was beginning to be economically successful, some labor leaders began demanding security for workers who were handicapped or unemployed. Because it seemed an economical way to avoid the kind of inconvenience these problems posed, many employers were quite willing for the government to assume this responsibility. The people of Great Britain had no illusions about this kind of support bridging the difference between classes. They simply endorsed the idea that the state supported those unfortunate enough to be without income only to keep them from becoming too troublesome. After World War I, a grateful nation accorded other rights to those who had served in the war. Strikes were not acceptable, but there was more movement toward socialization of some major industries and, perhaps most important, of the medical profession.

Not until after World War II did either of these become reality. By that time Britons had had a taste of wartime equality. The people knew they had rights and were eager to claim them. After years of inadequate health care, the people of Britain felt it one of their greatest needs. Why should not the costs be borne by all the people? Why should not the government regulate health care? The British system is a landmark. Patients choose their physicians, visit them when they need to, and receive outpatient and inpatient hospital care at state expense. The system has been criticized—but more by outsiders than by participants. Some British citizens may complain about the lack of efficiency or the cost of the "National Health." They do not complain about having it. Most of these who complain live outside Britain and have not had firsthand knowledge of it.

Both major parties, Conservative and Labour, claim responsibility and credit for the National Health. Although it is admitted to have problems that need work, there is no suggestion in Britain that the National Health Plan be abandoned.

The area of social welfare was expanded considerably during and after World War II. With considerable revision and improvement, the Parliament eventually passed a law designating to "local authorities" most of the delivery of service jobs that had considerable input into the most recent regulations. Their familiarity with clients' problems led them to insist that clients be relieved of the necessity to move from one office to another, answering the same questions and getting the same referrals. The British now offer one of the most comprehensive social services to be found anywhere in the world, emanating from one agency, in most cases through one worker. Britain's smaller size encourages this centrality. In addition, British agencies called "Citizens Aid" are available in every locality to help interpret the law and assure all citizens their rights. Furthermore, a great variety of voluntary agencies exist to fill the cracks where they are perceived between needs and government services.

One fear has been that the welfare state will rob its citizens of motivation and encourage them to depend on welfare rather than make a living. A case in point may help dispel this fear. A young American was working as a caseworker in the Tooting district of South London. He received a letter from the sister of a woman living in the district. Ms. Beck was said to be eighty-seven years old, living alone, and in need of social services. Since she had no phone, the young caseworker, Harry, wrote suggesting an appointment the following week. On that day he arrived at her address, introduced himself to her downstairs neighbor who was expecting him, and mounted the three flights of stairs to Ms. Beck's room. She answered his knock and invited him into the room, which was dusty and cluttered but basically clean. She seemed confused about the reason for his visit. He explained that he had been told that she might be in need of some social services and proceeded to suggest someone who could do her shopping, homemaker service, meals on wheels, and, finally, referral to a general practitioner. Ms. Beck's response was tart and to the point. She did her own shopping at the shops just down the road. She cooked what she liked when she liked and needed no help with meals. As for the physician, she had "not been to a doctor since I was twenty-five and see no reason to start now." Ms. Beck lived on her pension and felt no need to have someone help her do it. Harry agreed that she was doing fine but told her where she could reach him if she wanted to. They parted on good terms.

Ms. Beck is hardly the traditional recipient of welfare benefits. She was not seeking employment and probably never would. But like unemployed people everywhere, she preferred to be independent.

In Britain, the unemployment rate varies from north to south. It is much higher in the north. Those who are unemployed receive unemployment compensation. Like most workers the world over, they actively seek work and willingly give up unemployment compensation in favor of a job.

Not all British people feel like Ms. Beck. Many of them feel they have a right to welfare services when they need them, just as they have a right to their excellent public libraries, their schools, parks, and museums. Certainly not everyone needs or uses all these services all the time. But they are available to be used when needed. Why should one service carry more stigma than others?

Switzerland

In contrast to Great Britain and many other European countries, Switzerland has a tradition of independence and self-reliance of its citizens. Small, landlocked, and devoid of many natural resources, it is now one of the world's wealthiest countries. Swiss culture is many-faceted. Some of its twenty-five cantons are German-speaking, some French, some Italian; and in the Grissons, a fourth language, Romansch, is spoken. Further, some cantons are primarily Roman Catholic, some are Protestant, and some are a mixture. Politically, all of Switzerland is quite conservative. No one suggests that it is a welfare state. Nevertheless, health insurance, old-age pensions, and unemployment insurance at least are provided to most of the population through private insurance companies. Insurance is required by the state for all employed persons, and Switzerland has only a 1 percent unemployment rate.

The federal constitution requires some very specific coverage and leaves a great deal more up to the canton and local government. For example, the federal government requires that churches be supported by taxation. Yet Swiss citizens may choose to pay this tax or not. The federal government requires that all workers pay for health insurance through private companies. Yet private companies rather than government taxes were approved by the citizens in a plebiscite (vote). The Swiss regard full employment as a right, and when economic circumstances force some workers out of work, they are apt to be foreign workers who can be as easily exported as imported. To date, Swiss workers have felt very little effect of the international recession, though the Swiss government may well feel it.

Services are generally provided by the canton or locality, but the federal constitution specifies which are to be required and which are allowed. Thus, as in most countries, urban affluent communities provide extensive services for children and families while rural, poor areas provide much less.

Switzerland addresses some of the services outlined by Kahn and Kammerman better than others. However, it seems clear that the Swiss are quite sophisticated in their preventive and support services. Swiss provision for offering daily living and growth supports for ordinary, average people (as described by Kahn and Kammerman) seems at first glance to be considerably less generous than that provided by the British. The cantons differ greatly in their provision of day care for preschool children, senior citizens centers, and family-planning services. Most cantons do not provide nearly as much as the United Kingdom. However, health care and social security are well provided for by private insurance. Unemployment insurance is also provided for by private companies but is required by the federal government for all employed people. As we noted above, unemployment has not been a real problem in Switzerland, as it has in the United Kingdom. The provision of five months' unemployment insurance has so far been quite adequate. In 1975 a plebiscite was taken to determine whether the state should take over insurance. The people voted overwhelmingly to keep the present system of required private insurance.

Kahn and Kammerman list disseminating information about, and facilitating access to, services and entitlements anywhere in the social sector as the second task of a sophisticated social service system. In Canada, as in the United States, historically, seeking help carries a stigma. In Britain, Citizens Advice Bureaus are readily available to help citizens through the bureaucratic process. In Switzerland, social services are attached to and part of various other agencies including churches and industries. People in need of advice and information on how to get services receive them from these sources rather than from government agencies. The end result seems to be the same.

The third task listed by Kahn and Kammerman was "assuring for the frail aged, the handicapped, the retarded, and the incapacitated a basic level of social care and aid necessary to support functioning in the community or in substitute living arrangements." Here the Swiss federal government, like the British and Canadian, intervenes directly. Likewise, the government arranges substitute home or residential care or creates new permanent family relationships for children whose parents are not able to fulfill their roles.

The Swiss, with their private voluntary agencies, many subsidized by the government, have generally achieved much the same kinds of service delivery as the British with their much more socialized system. With their heterogeneous population and differences in language, religion, and economy, the Swiss have managed to provide nearly the same kinds and degrees of services as have developed countries everywhere.

Summary

Three countries' systems have been selected to compare with the U.S. welfare systems. Great Britain provides the historical precedent for much of the U.S. provisions. It provides the most in personal services and has the lowest per capita income of the four. Switzerland is more oriented toward full employment than any of the others and provides required insurance. Canada is the nearest to the United States and the most comparable in geographic size. It is much more sparsely populated, and like the United States and Switzerland, has a three-tier government system. Like the United States, its welfare system is in transition, neither comprehensive nor federally organized.

All three of the countries discussed provide family allowances and comprehensive hospitalization and health care, unlike the United States.

Notes

1. Alfred Kahn and Sheila Kammerman, *Social Services in International Perspective* (Washington, D.C.: U.S. Department of Health, Education, and Welfare, 1977), p. 2.

2. Kahn and Kammerman, *Social Services*, p. 5.

3. Eileen Younghusband, "Intercultural Aspects of Social Work," in *The Practice of Social Work*, eds. Klenk and Ryan (Belmont, Calif.: Wadsworth Publishing, 1970), pp. 36–37.

11

SOME IMPLICATIONS
FOR THE FUTURE
OF SOCIAL WORK

In looking at history, we see that a variety of systems, as well as subsystems and supersystems, affect each other and bring about changes in the process of social work. From a charity or residual system to a social welfare or institutional system in both the United States and England seems in retrospect to be a very logical, and predictable, process. Only with hindsight, however, can this process be determined. When we look at the future it is much more difficult to see either short-range or long-range developments. At the same time we must recognize that the vicissitudes of economics, politics, and religion are compounded by their interrelationships with each other, as with new and previously unconsidered changes in ecology, demography, and population growth, to mention only a few. Planned change must always recognize the reality that unplanned change is a real part of life.

Nevertheless, we must try to predict some things in both the short run and the long run, for the sake of practitioners who are already in the field of social work, and for students who wish to know whether or not the field is one in which they are likely to succeed.

First, let us hypothesize that social work is a profession that is likely to be around for some time to come. This seems likely despite what has become known as backlash sentiment in the entire field of social welfare. Social welfare legislation has rarely been repealed, once enacted. The social security laws, long overdue, difficult to administer, and inadequate as they were and are, have not been seriously questioned ever since they were enacted in 1935. Even the most fiscally conservative campaigners in their appeals to irate tax-payers have not suggested that the United States would be better off under a system of voluntary charity for the poor. Old-age insurance, unemployment insurance, and assistance for certain categories of dis-ability, including families of dependent children, are now part of U.S. life. Increases in social security payments, expansion of the regula-tions to include even limited medical care, and a proposal for guaran-teed income have all met with resistance and loud protests against "socialism," but no one has suggested that earlier efforts toward "so-cialism" be taken away. For whatever reason—religious, economic, political, or something else—social legislation, once enacted, seems to persist.

Social work as a profession has found, too, that there are a number of practice settings that have grown rapidly in the past decade. One of these is industrial social work or employee assistance plans. For-merly known as industrial social work, it means the employment of social workers by industry. In 1978 there were fewer than 100 in the nation. In 1985 there were nearly 4,000 members in a national profes-sional organization. One reason for this growth must be the lack of public welfare programs, but another must be that employers are in-creasingly aware of and concerned about the many kinds of problems that confront their employees. Whether or not they are employment related, they affect production.

Another example of a new setting is work with the aging, a need clearly evident in view of the aging of the U.S. population.

Social work in health settings of many kinds—Health Mainte-nance Organizations, group practices, and public health organiza-tions—has moved a long way from the original hospital social worker.

The same systems that have been operative in the past in shaping social work will probably continue to be so. How can changes in the religious, economic, and political systems be expected to affect social work?

Religion

Two changes in the religious system in this country and in England have had considerable effect on the practice of social work. One is that the religious institutions have recognized that they have functions other than theological ones. Most churches nowadays have extensive programs of recreation, socialization, social welfare, and community action. Most churches feel a responsibility to take an active part in the everyday lives of the members, not just their Sunday lives. Middle-class church members have felt a need to go outside their normal church activities, outside their own suburbs. In large measure, they have been urged and encouraged in their social consciences by clergymen of all denominations, many of whom have led the way to community action far removed from pastoral duties. The freedom riders of the early 60s, the Pentagon sit-in in the mid-60s, and the poor people's march in the late 60s had a large component of clergy from all over the country. Thus, in many ways, the churches have led community participation for community action.

The second change in the religious system is that many of the previously accepted norms and values are no longer universally accepted. Marriage and family mores are changing. So are many of the concepts related to law and order. Civil disobedience became acceptable in the 1960s, but the 1970s and 1980s brought such a confusion of public wrongs in high places as to make sit-ins and protests somewhat parochial matters. The whole question of law and order has been replaced by the concept of individual personal responsibility, at least in some circles. The thought of an authority who decides right and wrong, reward and punishment, is antithetical to many people, particularly to many young people. Having discarded the need for a deity to take care of them, these people have turned to humanistic values. They feel the need for closer relationships with people. Relationship is a time-honored social work concept that, as Biestek pointed out, involves acceptance, a nonjudgmental attitude, confidentiality, self-determination, individualization, purposeful expression of feeling, and controlled emotional involvement. None of these refers to authority, law-making, or even the Ten Commandments. As more people recognize more need for satisfying relationships, understanding and use of these relationships may become the most important concepts for all people, not just those in the helping professions.

Ironically, the opportunities for satisfying relationships are few and far between.

Modern industrial society tends to destroy and not to build relationships. Technological developments require shifts in occupation and changes in living environments. There is no identity, or relationship on a personal basis with a monopolized industry, a large company, or the society as a whole, represented by the tax gatherer, and police. There being no relationship, there is no motivation for observing the rules. This is a situation that will get even worse as industrial society gets larger and even more anonymous. The "outsider" and the "dropout" now comprise a growing subculture.

At the same time industrial society makes greater demands on its members, it is competitive, its luxuries become necessities, and its inequalities provide a motivation for types of behavior which defies its property-based norms. Furthermore, our cultural goals include acquisition and success measured by wealth. . . . The two factors, the absence of relationships that if present would promote conformity and the presence of pressures that motivate deviance, together ensure an increasing level of organized crime, for relationships can be developed within a criminal subculture, thus satisfying a basic human need. The norms of this subculture are policed, as in the wider society, by the value its members attach to relationships within. Thus all its members are required to observe norms of violence against the wider society from which they feel rejected.

This quotation is from an address by Dr. John Burton, Director of the Center for the Analysis of Conflict, University of London, made to the British Association for Social Workers, October 25, 1973. Dr. Burton's thesis is that law and order and institutional norms are in themselves examples of structural violence that individuals are fighting against. Because there is no longer universal acceptance of these norms, people find themselves in greater need than ever of close personal relationships. To give some concrete examples: Marriage and the family are no longer accepted as the only lifestyles available to people. Alternatives include communal living, unmarried couples living together, and homosexual couples living together. None of these was a public possibility in the white middle-class culture twenty years ago. Even today legal prohibitions against some or all of them exist in some places. Nevertheless, they are now viable alternatives. People who choose marriage and family are no longer bound by law or by public opinion to stay married for life. Parents are still legally responsible for their children, but not *all* parents are responsible, and increasingly this responsibility is accepted by the state.

The 1980's have brought a return to conservative materialism on the part of religious and political organizations. Still, many people remain unconvinced. The moral majority have not become either moral nor a majority.

Economics

Economically, all countries, including England, Canada, and the United States, have felt the effect of ever-increasing inflation. In brief, inflation means that money becomes worth less in terms of buying real goods. In times of inflation, the people who suffer most are those on fixed incomes. When these incomes are fixed at a very low level, as with welfare recipients, the suffering is acute. But since the inflation affects all sectors of the economy, governments are not likely to remedy the situation by increasing welfare or social security grants.

As the economic situation in the United States has improved—unemployment is down, inflation is down—the tremendous gap between the rich and the poor has become more obvious. The federal government, through the first five years of the 1980s, has systematically cut social programs affecting the poor while refusing tax increases for the well-to-do. Tax breaks continue to help those who pay large taxes. People whose income is not taxable do not reap any tax advantages. The tax reform of 1986 will provide the best relief for those whose income is currently taxed at 50 percent.

The proposed help for catastrophic illness will help very few elderly people since it does not provide for nursing home nor home care—only for hospitalization.

Politics

People on welfare have been further affected by the conservative, big-business orientation of presidential administrations that have held to the notion that rising costs and shortages will eventually right themselves if left alone. The government's concern for business interests rather than consumer interests gives little hope for relief for those consumers who are farthest down the list. Given the government's reluctance to act on behalf of the poor, two possible results may be looked for.

First, the position of very poor people may become so bad as to render them nearly helpless as well as hopeless, and their numbers may become expanded to the point that unemployment is a fact for great numbers of U.S. citizens. As in other times and in other countries, the poor may simply accept their fate and, like the conservative government, wait for times to get better. The second possibility is that this generation of poor people may be unwilling to accept their fate. Experience with some degree of self-determination during previous decades may encourage them to take a second route. They may organize, demonstrate, and protest. Whether or not they can be successful remains to be seen. A frightened and deprived population may react differently to a war on poverty from an affluent society.

Given either of these possible courses of action, what will be the posture of social work? Will social workers line up with the clients or will they feel that their role is that of mediator or broker between the oppressed and the oppressors who are not much better off? No answers can be given. But social work's relatively new position of change agent would seem to indicate that the profession will need to move beyond earlier efforts in times of economic and political recession. If social workers are committed to changing the system and affecting public policy, they will surely not be satisfied with applying band-aids on the worst of the social ills and ignoring the rest.

In the United States the 1976 elections brought a change from Republican to Democratic leadership. While the new administration promised welfare reform, the consensus of government representatives is that reform will be a long, slow process. In a *New York Times* article, May 22, 1977, David Rosenbaum points out that the government must constantly fight prevailing welfare myths. Despite masses of evidence to the contrary, there is widespread belief in the stereotype of "the lazy shiftless adult who could lift himself from the dole if he did not prefer to spend his days lolling on street corners and his nights procreating."[1] In fact, welfare is limited almost entirely to children and their mothers. A 1977 study by the Rand Corporation in California showed that 65 percent of all welfare mothers in that state had children under six. Those without small children, the study found, were "substantially underschooled, undertrained, and underskilled."[2]

Rosenbaum goes on to cite another myth—that "cheating on welfare is rampant and that the government would be better advised to round up absent fathers and make them support their families rather than simply pay relief to their dependents."[3] In fact, the best estimates of welfare cheating place the number at 5 to 10 percent of the recipients—certainly much less prevalent than cheating on income tax or on expense accounts. Finding absent fathers has been tried by some states. The results are expensive and unsatisfactory.

The third myth—that once people become poor they remain poor—has also been shown false. The poor population is extremely fluid. Finally, it is widely believed that poor blacks leave southern states with low welfare payments to go to New York for the better welfare benefits. In fact, most migrants go to cities for better job opportunities and wages. Migrants are less likely to go on welfare than blacks who were born in the cities.

All of this information is cited because it supports our earlier statements and because it points up the complexity of welfare reform. How can the best-intentioned administration reform an institution when most of the population is misinformed about the institution?

We must try to predict some possible developments in the field of social welfare and in the social work profession. We must do this both for the sake of current practitioners and for the sake of students who need to have some feel for the future of their chosen field.

We have seen that nothing happens in a vacuum, and certainly this is true of the political-economic developments of the 1980s. When the Republican party came into power in 1980, there was talk of a political mandate—a taxpayers' revolt. This revolt, begun as passage of Proposition 13 in California, suggested that people nationwide were in favor of tax and budget cuts. These cuts were promised by the Reagan administration. Not surprisingly, some services must be cut to provide budget cuts. Not surprisingly, human services, including the sacrosanct social security provisions, have been among the first to be cut. If services are cut, so inevitably are social work positions; even those in the private sector are funded directly or indirectly by tax monies. The plan of making block grants to states will hardly be helpful to those workers whose services are being cut, whether the programs are state or federal.

In February 1987, the *NASW News* published a list of principles for welfare reform endorsed by the National Association of Social Workers and ninety other organizations. The principles are:

- Persons who work should be rewarded for their efforts. They should receive income sufficient to support a family and access to necessary health care and child care. Barriers to the employment of low-income persons should be eliminated.

- Job opportunities, job counseling, training, education, placement, and supportive services should be widely available as primary tools to prevent and overcome poverty.

- The federal government should assure a minimum standard of living—including sufficient food, clothing, shelter, and medical care—to those in poverty.

- Additional investments should be made in programs proved successful in preventing future poverty and its ill effects.

- Welfare policies should aid both one- and two-parent families in need. Existing child-support laws should be more effectively enforced.

- In achieving the objectives above, the federal government should maintain a strong presence, setting minimum benefit standards, providing adequate resources for effective programs, and supporting appropriate and effective state and local initiatives.[4]

These organizations do not follow the administration's thinking. Their question is not *whether* welfare families can be brought into the labor force but *how* this can be done.

Late in 1985, Congress passed the Balanced Budget and Emergency Deficit Control Act, commonly known as Gramm-Rudman-Hollings, which mandated cuts in federal government spending to relieve the budget deficit. Domestic programs of all kinds will be most affected, and programs for the poor will be cut drastically over a period of years. Even though parts of the bill have been declared unconstitutional, initial cuts in March 1986 will affect children's programs adversely. While it is too early to foresee all the ramifications, it is reasonable to predict that children, who make up 40 percent of the poor, will continue to be separated from the more affluent society.

With federal programs cut and a similar fate facing state and local programs, it would seem reasonable to depend more on voluntary giving. Ironically, tax cuts make it more expensive to be philanthropic. A study by the Urban Institute found that "a reduction in tax rates, especially for those in the upper tax brackets, will result in what is called a higher price of giving."[5]

The *Independent Sector*, which commissioned the Urban Institute study, reports that "because charitable contributions are deductible from income in computing tax obligations, it does not really cost those who itemize their deductions full dollar to contribute a dollar to charity."[6] The report ends with a warning: "In the present case our projections suggest a period of considerable economic stringency and decline for a wide range of private, nonprofit charitable institutions. If by identifying this probable outcome this report helps trigger the changes in behavior needed to avert it, it will have served a useful purpose. What should be clear, however, is that these changes will have to be substantiated."[7]

In view of the likelihood of severe budget cuts for human services, which probably cannot and will not be made up in the private sector, what is the fate of social welfare and social work?

First of all, the needy will not vanish because services are scarcer. Unemployment among some segments of the population—notably black males—is higher in the mid-1980s than it was in the early 1980s. The contrast is greater because employment for white males and females improved.

In every city—not just New York City and Chicago—homelessness is a very real and growing problem. The Community Mental Health systems of the 1960s and 70s have not fulfilled their promise. Up to 50 percent of today's homeless people may be mentally ill. In addition, a very new kind of homeless population is growing, namely families of people who have lost jobs, farms, homes, who find themselves without resources and without much hope.

In the May–June 1985 issue of *Social Work*, Carol Meyer, Editor-in-Chief, wrote:

> The people of this country are being controlled by the government's devastating foreign and fiscal policies, the intent of which seems to be the destruction of what is left of the American values of generosity, compassion and social consciousness. The Administration's budgetary decisions to demolish welfare, job training, child care, student loans, programs in education and the arts, family farms, small businesses, housing and even Amtrak are so outrageous that one would be shocked if Congress and the American people would tolerate them. The arms build-up in light of the threat of nuclear extinction and lack of clear danger of attack from anywhere, seems to be a charade whose goal is a return to the pre-New Deal social structure. This goal has been

on the agenda of the far right since the passage of the social security act and piece by piece, it looks as if it will be achieved.[8]

Meyer goes on to say:

It is clear what the Reagan Administration is doing, presumably having been reelected by the American people to do it. It is not clear what social workers are thinking and doing about it all. The government policies and the rising punitiveness are related, of course, as are public attitudes toward the homeless, people with AIDS, the poor, and all oppressed minorities. The rush to consumerism, survival of the fittest, and the loss of community and caring will have their consequences. Perhaps in the pursuit of self-interest, the American people will lose even the purpose and meaning of society itself . . . a sense of social responsibility is not innate; it must be created through choice and nurtured and fought for whenever it is threatened. Social workers should be on the front lines of the battle to choose social responsibility and a sense of community over self-interest.

More than other administrations to date, under Ronald Reagan the current Republicans are dedicated to restructuring the welfare state through privatization. As Mimi Abramovitz has written in "The Privatization of the Welfare State: A Review," this is not a new practice.[9] Still, the practice of giving business and industry a chance to profit from expanding government services is a way of creating a new two-class welfare system. Privatization "allows the private sector to 'serve' the least costly, least troublesome and potentially most treatable clients." In so doing, the poorest and multiproblemed clients are left with meager, stigmatic public programs.

As early as October 1981, NASW's President Mary Ann Quaranta, and the board of directors, recommended that NASW "develop a system of data gathering and analysis so that it is in a stronger position to disseminate information." In another article in the same issue of NASW News, the strategy for collecting data is explained. Public hearings will be required of all states' requisition block grants, and social workers are urged to collect data on service needs to substantiate their claims. The hope is that hard evidence as to need will receive considerable attention from the media, and that this evidence will have an effect on decisions about the provisions of social services at both federal and state levels. There is no assurance that evidence of need will turn the tide in the erosion of human services, but leaders of the profession are aware of a need to fight for themselves, their clients, and the eroding services, and they have worked out a strategy for addressing this need.

The establishment of coalitions is another strategy for calling attention to unmet needs. Coalitions of organizations with like commitments have been in use for a number of years, but NASW hopes to promote existing ones and develop new ones.

Development of members' political potential is another, greatly needed strategy. Social workers have not been notably successful in running for or holding public office. Still, some social workers in the past have made noticeable impact on people in power. Harry Hopkins' influence on Franklin Roosevelt must have been similar to David Stockman's on Ronald Reagan.

In a paper presented at the Society for the Study of Social Problems, Toronto, Canada, in August 1981, James Fendrich and Douglas St Angelo predict:

> Even if all the questionable supply-side assumptions about investment are granted, the trickle-down theory is a very costly way to generate jobs. The Reagan administration is predicting 3 million jobs will result from the $750 billion tax cuts. That is more than $200,000 for every job. In contrast, CETA jobs cost less than $10,000 and other public works jobs cost less than $50,000.[10]

On the basis of the British experience with supply-side economics, Fendrich and St Angelo foresee quite the opposite effects from those predicted. In Britain, tax cuts for the wealthy have not produced more jobs. "Instead, unemployment has increased. Corporations on the verge of bankruptcy have had to borrow more, not less. There have been two major tax cuts for the wealthy; however, industrial output is falling at an almost unprecedented rate."[11]

These authors predict dire consequences. Only the advent of a major international war would provide justification for the expansion of the federal budget and the national debt.

From quite another and longer range view the National Association of Social Workers Professional Futures Commission published four scenarios in the September 1981 issue of *Social Work*.[12] Using the concepts of postindustrialization articulated by sociologist Daniel Bell and of transformationalism articulated by humanist and social scientist Willis Harmon, the scenarios postulate two possibilities—one "sweet" and one "sour" in each of the postindustrial and transformationalist approaches. In the postindustrial sweet scenario, the energy problem is solved, the United States has a thriving service economy characterized by computer technology. Social work would be divided into narrow specializations; the prevailing mode of service delivery would be third-party payments rather than private practice or agency practice. Because most material needs would be met through technology, the demand for social philosophers would be even less than it is now. Society would be ordered, peaceful, and well supplied materially. Social workers might find it regimented and technological—but not bad.

The sour aspect of the postindustrial scenario shows environmental and health problems unsolved by technology. Gradual drift to the right brings oppression and a kind of international fascism. Social work might well fall in with a scheme to superorganize or overorganize social services when the government supplies block grants to every county and every urban community. Isolation of the deviant— whatever their deviance—makes custodians of some social workers but gives others an opportunity to work in the area of prevention. "Social workers begin to pride themselves on their ability to prevent," Daniel Bell envisions, "even though they are unable to say precisely what they are preventing or by what methods."

The "sweet" scenario of the transformational school posits a society in change. The emergence of a new party with strong international counterparts brings about concern for environmental and energy conservation. Community development corporations organize to pool local resources for food production, employment, and other essential activities. They concern themselves with social and physical well-being, using self-help, mutual aid, and consumer cooperatives to further their goals. With the demise of bureaucracy, another network emerges, composed of analogous segments of various sizes. They are decentralized, multiheaded, and ideological. Social work as a profession is neither affordable nor needed. People have learned to help themselves.

The transformational "sour" scenario posits the occurrence of a catastrophe, possibly a nuclear accident or nuclear war. With no people's party to sanction the networking, various groups band together seeking the help of gurus. Social work, through NASW chapters, organizes volunteer efforts. Gradually a new society begins to form, but without a power base the communal groups become increasingly separate. Conflict bred of lack of resources and productivity results in the emergence of a reactionary third force. Brutal repressive fascism takes over, making social services obsolete, and the profession of social work is no more.

The authors conclude that all the scenarios point up certain common truths. First, the necessity for being global minded—the future of this country is inextricably connected with that of the rest of the world, including the developing countries. Second, the profession of social work may not be as important to preserve as the integrity of society. If people truly are able to help themselves, social workers should surely rejoice, not complain. The author says:

> Lest the future histories presented here prove to contain a grain of truth, it is necessary for social work to keep alive its fundamental commitments and act upon them; to avoid putting the well-being of the profession over the well-being of people; to be on the alert to the signs of the growing darkness around us and to stand ready to struggle and fight—and perhaps to lose—on the basis of cause rather than capitulate and accommodate on the basis of function.[13]

Notes

1. David Rosenbaum, "Officials Are Up against the Myths of Welfare," *New York Times*, May 22, 1977, p. 70.

2. Rosenbaum, "Officials Are Up."

3. Rosenbaum, "Officials Are Up."

4. Harris, Dorothy, "Finding Alternatives to Reagan's Welfare-Reform Arguments," *NASW News* 32, no. 2 (February 1987).

5. "Charitable Giving Could Wilt When It's Needed Most," *NASW News* 26, no. 9 (October 1981).

6. "Charitable Giving."

7. "Charitable Giving."

8. Carol Meyer, Editorial, *Social Work*, May–June 1985.

9. Abramovitz, "The Privatization of the Welfare State: A Review," *Social Work* 31, no. 4 (July–August 1986), p. 257.

10. James Fendrich and Douglas St Angelo, "The Reagan Election and Mandates: Their Fiscal Policy Implications for the Welfare State." Unpublished paper, October 1981.

11. Fendrich and St Angelo, "The Reagan Election."

12.   National Association of Social Workers Professional Futures Commission.

13.   Bertram Beck, "Social Work's Future: Triumph or Disaster?" *Social Work* 26, no. 5 (September 1981), p. 367.

APPENDIX A

NATIONAL ASSOCIATION OF SOCIAL WORKERS (NASW) CODE OF ETHICS

1. **THE SOCIAL WORKER'S CONDUCT AND COMPORTMENT AS A SOCIAL WORKER**

    A. *Propriety.* The social worker should maintain high standards of personal conduct in the capacity or identity as social worker.
    B. *Competence and professional development.* The social worker should strive to become and remain proficient in professional practice and the performance of professional functions.
    C. *Service.* The social worker should regard as primary the service obligation of the social work profession.
    D. *Integrity.* The social worker should act in accordance with the highest standards of professional integrity.
    E. *Scholarship and research.* The social worker engaged in study and research should be guided by the conventions of scholarly inquiry.

2. **THE SOCIAL WORKER'S ETHICAL RESPONSIBILITY TO CLIENTS**

    F. *Primacy of clients' interests.* The social worker's primary responsibility is to clients.
    G. *Rights and prerogatives of clients.* The social worker should make every effort to foster maximum self-determination on the part of clients.
    H. *Confidentiality and privacy.* The social worker should respect the privacy of clients and hold in confidence all information obtained in the course of professional service.
    I. *Fees.* When setting fees, the social worker should ensure that they are fair, reasonable, considerate, and commensurate with the service performed and with due regard for the clients' ability to pay.

3. **THE SOCIAL WORKER'S ETHICAL RESPONSIBILITY TO COL-LEAGUES**

   J. *Respect, fairness, and courtesy.* The social worker should treat colleagues with respect, courtesy, fairness, and good faith.

   K. *Dealing with colleagues' clients.* The social worker has the responsibility to relate to the clients of colleagues with full professional consideration.

4. **THE SOCIAL WORKER'S ETHICAL RESPONSIBILITY TO EMPLOY-ERS AND EMPLOYING ORGANIZATIONS**

   K. *Commitments to employing organizations.* The social worker should adhere to commitments made to the employing organizations.

5. **THE SOCIAL WORKER'S ETHICAL RESPONSIBILITY TO THE SO-CIAL WORK PROFESSION**

   M. *Maintaining the integrity of the profession.* The social worker should uphold and advance the values, ethics, knowledge, and mission of the profession.

   N. *Community service.* The social worker should assist the profession in making social services available to the general public.

   O. *Development of knowledge.* The social worker should take responsibility for identifying, developing, and fully utilizing knowledge for professional practice.

6. **THE SOCIAL WORKER'S ETHICAL RESPONSIBILITY TO SOCIETY**

   P. *Promoting the general welfare.* The social worker should promote the general welfare of society.

APPENDIX B

AN INTERNATIONAL CODE OF ETHICS

At the International Federation of Social Workers General Meeting in San Juan, Puerto Rico, July 10, 1976, the delegates adopted an International Code of Ethics for the Professional Social Worker, which follows:

Social work originates variously from humanitarian, religious and democratic ideals and philosophies and has universal application to meet human needs arising from personal-societal interactions and to develop human potential. Professional Social Workers are dedicated to service for the welfare and self-fulfillment of human beings; to the development and disciplined use of scientific knowledge regarding human and societal behavior; to the development of resources to meet individual, group, national and international needs and aspirations, and to the achievement of social justice.

PRINCIPLES
1. Every human being has a unique value, irrespective of origin, ethnicity, sex, age, beliefs, social and economic status or contribution to society.
2. Each individual has the right of self-fulfillment to the degree that it does not encroach upon the same right of others.
3. Each society, regardless of its form, should function to provide the maximum benefits for all of its members.
4. The professional Social Worker has the responsibility to devote objective and disciplined knowledge and skill to aid individuals, groups, communities, and societies in their development and resolution of personal-societal conflicts and their consequences.
5. The professional Social Worker has a primary obligation to the objective of service, which must take precedence over self-interest aims or views.

STANDARDS OF ETHICAL CONDUCT

General

1. Seek and understand the worth of each individual and the elements which condition behavior and the service required.
2. Uphold and advance the values, knowledge and methodology of the profession, refraining from any behavior which damages the functioning of the profession.
3. Clarify all public statements or actions whether on an individual basis or as a representative of a professional association, agency or organization.
4. Recognize professional and personal limitations, encourage the utilization of all relevant knowledge and skills and apply scientific methods of inquiry.
5. Contribute professional expertise to the development of sound policies and programs to better the quality of life in each society.
6. Identify and interpret the social needs, the basis and nature of individual, group, community, national and international social problems, and the work of the social work profession.

Relative to clients

1. Maintain the client's right to a relationship of mutual trust, to privacy and confidentiality, and to responsible use of information. The collection and sharing of information or data shall only be related to the professional service function to be performed with the client informed as to its necessity and use. No information shall be released without prior knowledge and informed consent of the client, except where the client cannot be responsible or others may be seriously jeopardized.
2. Recognize and respect the individual goals, responsibilities, and differences of clients. Within the scope of the agency and the client's social milieu, the professional service shall assist clients to take responsibility for personal actions and to help all clients with equal willingness. Where the professional service cannot be provided under such conditions the client shall be so informed in such a way as to leave the client free to act.
3. Help the client—individual, group, community, or society—to achieve self-fulfillment and maximum potential within the limits of the equal rights of others. The service shall be based upon helping the client to understand and use the professional relationship, in furtherance of the client's legitimate desires and interests.

Relative to agencies and organizations

1. Work or cooperate with those agencies and organizations whose policies, procedures, and operations are directed toward adequate service delivery and encouragement of professional practice consistent with the Code of Ethics.

2. Responsibly execute the stated aims and functions of the agency or organization, contributing to the development of sound policies, procedures, and practice in order to obtain the best possible standards of service.
3. Sustain ultimate responsibility to the client, initiating desirable alterations of policy, procedures, and practice through appropriate agency and organizational channels. If necessary remedies are not achieved after channels have been exhausted, initiate appropriate appeals to higher authorities or the wider community of interest.
4. Insure professional accountability to client and community for efficiency and effectiveness through periodic review of client, agency and organizational problems and self-performance.

Relative to colleagues

1. Respect the training and performance of colleagues and other professionals extending all necessary cooperation that will enhance effective services.
2. Respect differences of opinion and practice of colleagues and other professionals expressing criticism through appropriate channels in a responsible manner.
3. Promote and share opportunities for knowledge, experience, and ideals with all professional colleagues, other professionals and volunteers for the purpose of mutual improvement and validation.
4. Bring any violations of client interest or professional ethics and standards to the attention of the appropriate bodies and defend colleagues against unjust actions.

Relative to the profession

1. Maintain the values, knowledge and methodology of the profession and contribute to their clarification and improvement.
2. Uphold the professional standards of practice and work for their advancement.
3. Defend the profession against unjust criticism and work to increase confidence in the necessity for professional practice.
4. Encourage new approaches and methodologies needed to meet new and existing needs.

APPENDIX C

THREE CASE STUDIES

1. TOMMY EDWARDS

The following case study shows the process of direct intervention involving a family, an individual, a group, and a larger community.

Tommy Edwards, a nine-year-old Caucasian boy attending fourth grade in a kindergarten through fourth-grade school that covered a district with a wide socioeconomic range, was referred to the school social worker and described as a constant classroom troublemaker. Most of the following information was obtained from the principal.

Although Tommy tested in the average range of intelligence, he had never done well in school. His parents were both deaf, and his mother was also mute. She was known to go into rages at neighborhood children and their parents when she thought they were making fun of her or picking on Tommy. She frequently thought Tommy was abused in normal interaction in play and seemed somewhat overprotective and lacking in knowledge of normal childhood development. When she was angry, she waved her arms and made faces in such a manner that the message of rage was clear. Tommy's father worked regularly as a janitor in a local hospital.

Their home, though shabby, was clean and fairly well-kept. The neighborhood, on the edge of an extremely affluent part of town, was run-down, dirty, and unkempt. Mrs. Edwards was isolated from most normal contacts in the neighborhood. One neighbor occasionally came over for coffee. Mrs. Edwards communicated by lip reading and writing. When she was annoyed with Tommy, she turned her back on him, which cut him off completely.

This unpublished case material is the property of Dr. Mary Jo Lockwood.

In school Tommy was inattentive, read poorly, and did not complete his work. His teacher, a middle-class woman with a traditional approach, had lost all patience with Tommy. She was merely lasting out the year, after which he would go to another school. She could not imagine Tommy ever fitting into her class. In observing the class, the worker felt that the teacher jumped on Tommy for errors she ignored in others. Tommy responded with stubbornness followed by tantrums and bad language.

The principal had tried several times to establish contact with Tommy's mother. She was unwilling to come to school for conferences and had been angry when the principal had visited. The principal and Tommy had a fairly good relationship. When Tommy was "sent to the office," the principal could calm him down quickly and had found that short periods of isolation were most effective in helping Tommy regain control of himself.

Tommy's father was a rather withdrawn person who seemed to be the dominant partner in the marriage. He and Tommy did very little together. He worked long hours, and Mrs. Edwards apparently turned to him for decisions. His hours made him difficult to interview. There was no extended family in town. Mrs. Edwards' sister lived about 100 miles away.

On the playground, Tommy was observed to play well with two or three other boys. He was well coordinated and enjoyed active play. He sometimes talked by moving his lips only and mispronounced many words. Tommy talked with the social worker casually one day in the office. He mentioned the fact that he badly wanted a dog. He had wanted to play Little League baseball, but had no way to get to the practice field as it was too far to walk and his father was not home by that time. The worker found him friendly.

The Edwards lived in a city of 500,000 with a number of social services. Church-going was an important part of the social life of the city. There was little public transportation. The city had an extensive recreation department and there was a park near the Edwards, with a swimming pool and a summer program. The school system had available psychologists (who usually tested); nurses, speech, reading and hearing consultants; and elementary teaching consultants. There was one class for emotionally disturbed children in the building. This school did not qualify for any special federal programs. There was an organization for the disabled that operated a day program of recreation and crafts and provided bus transportation nearby. Vocational rehabilitation was available through the Department of Welfare. There was a medical school in the city with a variety of outpatient clinics including an excellent children's psychiatric clinic for those children who were interesting teaching cases. There was a private family social service agency with a sliding fee scale.

Questions

1. Whom would you interview first? Why?
2. How would you begin?
3. Do you think you need all the background information? Why?
4. What kinds of feelings do you have about Tommy's mother? What kinds of feelings do you think the principal has about her?
5. What additional information do you need? Where would you get it?
6. With whom would you try to make contacts and for what purpose? List as many as you can, in order of priority.
7. What principles of relationship can you see applying to Tommy? To the principal of the school? To Tommy's mother?
8. As a school social worker, what would be your responsibility to your own agency? To the school? To Tommy?
9. What other agencies would you consider involving in this case?
10. As the school social worker involved, try writing a report on this case, beginning with the referral from the teacher. Use a planned change outline that will show the beginning, middle, and end of the case. Choose either a satisfactory or unsatisfactory solution but make clear the reasons for the outcome of the case.

2. LISA ENDER

The following case study shows the process of indirect intervention on the part of several community agencies, including the public school system.

Lisa Ender was the second child and second daughter of educated middle-class parents. Her only sister, Nancy, was seven years older and already diagnosed gifted when Lisa was born.

Lisa's birth was uneventful. She was an easy baby to live with, undemanding, and seemed to require a great deal of sleep. She was seen regularly by a pediatrician. When Lisa was not yet sitting alone by fourteen months, her doctor recommended that she be seen by a specialist. The diagnosis was developmental disability—reason unknown.

The Enders accepted this diagnosis reluctantly. They joined a parents' group and received considerable support and encouragement. By the time Lisa was four, a decision had to be made about her educational future. M City has a comprehensive preschool screening program, staffed by teams of social workers, psychologists, physicians, and teachers. They recommend children for special programs when indicated. Although Congress has approved such programs, not every state provides the service and not every locality within the state provides its. Funding comes from the localities.

Since Lisa at four was not yet speaking intelligibly, not yet toilet trained, and walked only with a walker, the need for a special program was evident. Of the two suggested, the one for physically handicapped children was favored by the physician. Children in this program receive extensive physical therapy, designed to help them maximize their limited abilities. Some of the children are in wheel chairs; some wear heavy braces and/or walk with crutches. Many, though not all, of these children have normal speaking and communication skills. Some are intellectually gifted, while some continue to show significant intellectual delays. The other program is for children whose intellectual development is slow. These children are stimulated by special education teachers to express themselves verbally, to feed themselves, and generally take care of their own needs. Both are operated by the school system.

Lisa's parents, after inspecting both, decided on the program for intellectually delayed children. Both programs operated half days for four-year-olds.

At the end of the year in the Whittier school program, Lisa had not made the kind of progress deemed necessary for admission to a normal kindergarten. Her parents admitted this. Her speech was incomprehensible. She moved with difficulty and related poorly with teachers and children. She was more or less toilet trained.

A conference of parents, teachers, and social workers provided varying views. Lisa's parents were still opposed to the physical therapy program. They felt she would not benefit from being with children more disabled than she. They objected to the image of physical handicap, maintaining that Lisa was merely "slow." The teacher who had worked with her all year felt that she was not nearly ready, physically or mentally, to deal with requirements even of a special kindergarten class. The other children, she felt, would make Lisa's life miserable because of her frequent bowel and bladder accidents, her stumbling, uncertain gait, and her lack of manual dexterity. The teacher was also convinced that the Whittier program had been an inappropriate placement during the past year and would continue to be an inappropriate placement for the coming year. The teacher's opinion was that Lisa's physical disabilities and extreme passiveness impacted so greatly on her performance in a school setting that she needed the greater one-to-one attention that she would receive at the physical therapy program. The social worker who had worked all year with Lisa's parents understood their fear of and bias against the medical atmosphere of the physical program. She could respect their fear that Lisa would not be challenged by the restrictive environment of a school for physically handicapped, frequently nonambulatory children. She accepted, though she did not necessarily concur, with the parents' proposal that Lisa remain at Whittier for a second year. By that time, the parents hoped that Lisa would be able to take her place in the lower third of the class and could attend a regular kindergarten class in her own neighborhood.

Since her diagnosis had never been revised, neither the physician nor the school administration were able or willing to make a different prognosis. Essentially, it seemed easier for the parents, at this point in Lisa's development, to acknowledge her intellectual delays (always with the hope that she would catch up) than to acknowledge her physical handicaps and admit that their child *belonged* in the physical therapy program.

For Lisa the decision was made to continue in the Whittier program for a second year. Both parents and school team understood that this might prove an unwise choice, and the school staff were especially aware that Lisa might well establish a precedent.

Lisa's future is still very doubtful. She will probably be a candidate for social services for some time to come. Her parents feel, with reason, that she and they have a right to these services. If their need is greater than others, so is their right.

Questions

1. What has the social worker's knowledge to do with this situation?
2. What systems are involved?
3. What skills has this social worker to use?
4. What values are evident?
5. Can you see a better solution for Lisa?

3. FRIENDSHIP GROUP

Thursday was group meeting day. Jean S. looked around the small room with the center table. Promptly at 2:00 P.M, eight second graders would arrive, ready for the day's therapy (no one, including the second graders, called it that). The group was designed as a preventive measure—insofar as prevention can take place at ages eight or nine. All over M City, social workers were following the same plan in different schools. The group's purpose was quite simple—to teach cooperation to children who did not understand the concept. The group's process was also quite simple—to give children tasks that would require cooperation.

What actually transpired was not so simple. First, the group members had to be identified. This was done by the second grade teachers who were encouraged to refer their "worst" students to the social worker. Not surprisingly, seven of the eight referrals were children who acted out, demanded attention, were troublemakers. One little girl was referred because of her extreme dependence, shyness, and lack of self-confidence.

Before the group was formed, the social worker interviewed both child and parents or guardian. The social worker explained the school's concern with children who had a hard time getting along with other children as well as with adults. Group membership was offered as a service to the family, a help to the child. Parental response was uneven—some parents were well aware of their children's problems and supplied considerable background information, while other parents were unaware of any problems. However, all were willing to permit membership in the group. To be sure that the children understood about the group, each was asked to tell what he or she thought was a problem, and then to make a contract with the social worker, an agreement to try certain kinds of behavior that might help solve the problem. The timid little girl suggested that she could be more independent in getting up and getting dressed in the morning, and in volunteering to read in school. Most of the children had difficulty in thinking of behaviors that they could try—since most perceived their problems to be caused by other children or teachers. Still, they came up with some ideas, which were duly recorded for further reference.

Group meetings lasted exactly one hour and were carefully structured. On arrival, each child was assigned a chair. No business started till each was seated. This took some time, as there was considerable pushing, shoving, and pinching, as well as many accusations and counteraccusations. When everyone was settled, the social worker asked each to tell the names of his or her fellow group members. For children who had been meeting for three months this seemed a very difficult task. Learning other people's names is a social skill not easily achieved, but important in fostering a desire for cooperation. The next item of business was a review of the contracts. This was done individually, though suggestions were encouraged from other group members. Each member was expected to recall the terms of his or her contract and to report details on progress or lack of progress. Since many had difficulty accepting responsibility for their behavior, the social worker was quite directive in insisting that they stay on the topic. This was complicated by the difficulty the other group members had with sitting quietly and listening. Each wanted to be the center of the worker's attention, not only in turn, but out of turn. Nonetheless, each child had a turn to report on his or her contract.

Next, it was time for the day's project. This decision required a new level of cooperation. The social worker offered two alternative activities—popsicle stick construction or collage making. Sometimes there was no consensus and the whole time was taken in trying to agree. This time, however, popsicle stick construction was a clear winner. Each child received a bundle of sticks, glue, and string. Not surprisingly, they were not very innovative. There was considerable copying, and even more bickering over whose string and whose glue was being used. Eventually, it was time to clean up and to review the meeting. Each child was encouraged to tell something positive that another had done at this meeting. The social worker added her comments. Then the meeting was over.

Second graders are not likely to acquiesce so easily to a structured meeting, and these second graders were more easily distracted, more restless, and more demanding than most. That is why they were there.

Questions

1. What purpose does Friendship Group have?
2. Do you think the rigid structure of the group meeting is helpful? Why?
3. Discuss the connection between the planned change process and this group process.
4. How much cooperation would you expect from teachers of these children? Why?

SELECTED
BIBLIOGRAPHY*

CHAPTER 1

Abbott, Edith. *Some American Pioneers in Social Welfare*. Chicago: University of Chicago Press, 1937. Biographical sketches of some important early social workers in the United States.

Abbott, Grace. *The Child and the State*. Chicago: University of Chicago Press, 1938. An early account of welfare programs for children.

Addams, Jane. *Twenty Years at Hull House*. New York: Macmillan, 1910. Miss Addams' own account of the early days in the settlement movement in Chicago.

Bartlett, Harriet M. "Toward Clarification and Improvement of Social Work Practice—A Working Definition of Social Work Practice." *Social Work* 3, no. 2 (1958), p. 3. An analysis of trends and issues in the thinking about social work practice.

Breckenridge, Sophonisba P. *Public Welfare Administration in the United States*. 3rd impression. Chicago: University of Chicago Press, 1935. A classic account of the United States' early efforts at welfare administration.

Collins, Alice H. *The Human Services: An Introduction*. Indianapolis: Odyssey Press, 1973. This book describes the tasks needed by human service workers and discusses the skills necessary to carry out these tasks.

Crampton, Helen M., and Kenneth K. Kaiser. *Social Welfare: Institution and Process*. New York: Random House, 1970. An easy-to-read, historical, and case study view of social welfare in the United States.

---

*Works cited in the chapters are not included in this bibliography.

Fink, Arthur E. *The Field of Social Work.* 6th ed. New York: Holt, Rinehart & Winston, 1974. A classic text that includes history, fields of practice methods, and many case studies.

Friedlander, Walter, and Robert Apte, eds. *Introduction to Social Welfare: Concepts and Methods in Social Work.* 6th ed. Englewood Cliffs, N.J.: Prentice-Hall, 1980. A comprehensive text covering nearly all aspects of social welfare and social work.

Gordon, William E. "A Critique of the Working Definition." *Social Work* 7 (July 4, 1962), p. 3. An article that expands, enlarges, and discusses the working definition proposed by Bartlett.

Harrington, Michael. *The Other America.* New York: Penguin Books, 1962. Reputed to be the book that sparked the war on poverty, it details some of the kinds of poverty to be found in the most affluent country in the world.

Johnson, H. Wayne. *The Social Services: An Introduction.* 2nd ed. Itasca, Ill.: F. E. Peacock Publishers, 1986. A new text on social work and social welfare.

Johnson, Louise. *Social Work Practice: A Generalist Approach.* 2nd ed. Boston: Allyn & Bacon, 1986. A process-oriented text on social work practice.

Klenk, Robert W., and Robert M. Ryan, eds. *The Practice of Social Work.* 2nd ed. Belmont, Calif.: Wadsworth Publishing, 1974. A book of readings by many well-known authors, using the social systems approach.

Miller, Henry. "Value Dilemmas in Social Casework." *Social Work* 13 (January 1968), p. 27. An article describing the kinds and degrees of value dilemmas faced by social workers.

Schulman, Eveline D. *Intervention in Human Services.* 2nd ed. St. Louis: C. V. Mosby, 1978. The second edition of a book on skills in human services.

Sheehan, Susan. *A Welfare Mother.* Boston: Houghton Mifflin, 1975. A case study of a real-life story of a woman on welfare.

Tripodi, Tony; Phillip Fellin; Irvin Epstein; and Roger Lind. *Social Workers at Work: An Introduction to Social Work Practice.* Itasca, Ill.: F. E. Peacock Publishers, 1972. A book of readings in the methods of casework, group work, and community work, with a section dealing with the profession of social work.

CHAPTER 2

Bennis, Warren G.; Kenneth D. Buene; and Robert Chin, eds. *The Planning of Change.* New York: Holt, Rinehart & Winston, 1969. A comprehensive book of readings covering planned change theory, systems theory, and strategies for implementation.

Berrien, T. Kenneth. *General and Social Systems.* New Brunswick, N.J.: Rutgers University Press, 1968. Applies general systems theory to problems in social psychology without dehumanizing those problems.

Boulding, Kenneth. "General Systems Theory: A Skeleton of Science." *Management Science* 12 (1956), p. 197. Outlines the general concepts required to view all of life systematically.

Hartman, Ann. "To Think About the Unthinkable." *Social Casework* 51 (October 1970), p. 467. A simply written article relating social work practice to systems theory.

Hearn, Gordon, ed. *The General Systems Approach: Contributions toward an Holistic Conception of Social Work.* New York: Council on Social Work Education, 1969. Promotes the development of a substantially inclusive, internally consistent, and organized conception of social work practice and its approach to the human scene.

Janchill, Sister Mary Paul. "Systems Concepts in Casework Theory and Practice." *Social Casework* 50 (February 1969), p. 74. An article that describes and defines systems theory terms in language familiar to social workers.

Parsons, Talcott. *The Social System.* New York: Free Press, 1951. A classic in social systems theory as an application of general systems theory.

Von Bertalanffy, Ludwig. "An Outline of General Systems Theory." *British Journal for the Philosophy of Science* 1 (1950), p. 134. A biological theory that provided the impetus for general systems theory.

CHAPTER 3

Bruce, Maurice. *The Rise of the Welfare State: English Social Policy 1601–1971.* London: Weidenfeld and Nicolson, 1973. A British publication describing and analyzing the history of welfare in that country.

Compton, Beulah. *Introduction to Social Welfare and Social Work—Structure, Function, and Process.* Chicago: Dorsey Press, 1980. An historical account of the development of social welfare and social work in the United States.

Dolgoff, Ralph, and Donald Feldstein. *Understanding Social Welfare.* New York: Harper & Row, 1980. This book describes the myths of American welfare, and provides an historical account of how they came into being.

Fedrico, Ronald C. *The Social Welfare Institution.* 3rd ed. Lexington, Mass.: D. C. Heath, 1980. A book that contains a history of social welfare as well as an approach to policy analysis and formulation.

Schenk, Quentin F., and Emmy Law Schenk. *Welfare, Society and the Helping Professions: An Introduction.* New York: Macmillan, 1981. This book documents and describes the relationships that exist between welfare programs and the society in which they are found.

Trattner, Walter I. *From Poor Law to Welfare State.* 2nd ed. New York: Free Press, 1979. An historical account of welfare in the United States, emphasizing the nineteenth and early twentieth centuries.

Zastrow, Charles. *Introduction to Social Welfare Institutions.* Rev. ed. Chicago: Dorsey Press, 1982. The history of social welfare is related to current social problems.

CHAPTER 4

Brammer, Laurence. *The Helping Relationship: Process and Skills.* Englewood Cliffs, N.J.: Prentice-Hall, 1979.

Cohen, Ruth. "Outreach and Advocacy in the Treatment of the Aged." *Social Casework* 55 (May 1974), p. 271. An article describing three projects that demonstrate the value of maintaining older persons in the mainstream of community life.

Egan, Gerard. *Exercises in Helping Skills.* Monterey, Calif.: Brooks/Cole Publishing, 1982. A training manual designed to accompany the *Skilled Helper*, though it is useful alone.

Fox, Evelyn, et al. "The Termination Process: A Neglected Dimension in Social Work." *Social Work* 14 (October 1969), p. 53. An article that discusses relevant theory, the reasons for termination, and an extensive clinical example of a twelve-year-old girl, based on observations through a one-way mirror during five therapy sessions, to point up the important aspects of the process, the client's feelings, and the worker's problems in helping the client work through termination.

Garrett, Annette. *Interviewing: Its Principles and Methods.* New York: Family Service Association of America, 1943. A classic book on social work interviewing, particularly for casework interviews.

Kadushin, Alfred. *Child Welfare Services: A Sourcebook.* New York: Crowell-Collier & Macmillan, 1970. A thorough and comprehensive book that describes the kinds and quality of services that have been offered to children in this country.

Kaufman, Irving. "Helping People Who Cannot Manage Their Lives." *Children* 13 (May–June 1966), p. 93. A psychiatrist discusses the kinds of character disorders that call for intervention outside the classic intrapsychic methods of treatment. He uses the term *emotionally retarded* and suggests the implications of treating such people.

Miller, Sherod; Elam Nunnally; and Daniel Wackman. *Alive and Aware*. Minneapolis: Interpersonal Communications Program, 1975. A manual for communication skills.

Oxley, Genevieve. "The Caseworker's Expectation and Client Motivation." *Social Casework* 47 (July 1966), p. 432. An article discussing the effect of positive and negative expectation by the caseworker on the role of the client in the casework process.

Shubert, Margaret. *Interviewing in Social Work Practice: An Introduction*. New York: Council on Social Work Education, 1971. A book enumerating factors affecting the interview, common types of interviews, and the dimensions that must be taken into account.

Smalley, Ruth. *Theory for Social Work Practice*. New York: Columbia University Press, 1967. A textbook outlining a common base for social work practice whether with individuals, groups, or communities.

Szasz, Thomas. *The Myth of Mental Illness*. New York: Harper & Row, 1961. One of the first of many books that question the medical basis of mental illness and posit the theory that illness and health are matters of opinion rather than fact.

CHAPTER 5

Ackerman, Nathan W. *Treating the Troubled Family*. New York: Basic Books, 1966. A book written by an acknowledged authority in the field of family therapy. The author discusses assessment, planning, and treatment from a systems orientation.

Ambrosino, Salvatore. "Integrating Counseling, Family Life Education, and Family Advocacy." *Social Casework* 60 (December 1979), pp. 579–85. Combining the three services establishes agency responsibility for families suffering from institutional injustices and gaps in services.

Billingsley, Andrew. *Black Families in White America*. Englewood Cliffs, N.J.: Prentice-Hall, 1968. A book giving a black perspective on families and how they live in this country.

Bracy, John J., et al. *Black Matriarchy: Myth or Reality*. Belmont, Calif.: Wadsworth Publishing, 1970. A book that disputes the stereotype of black culture as a matriarchy.

Hartman, Ann. "The Generic Stance and the Family Agency." *Social Casework* 55 (April 1974), p. 170. An article that expands the idea of an extended model of action, so that the client and all related systems are included.

Kent, Marilyn. "Remarriage: A Family Systems Perspective." *Social Casework* 61 (March 1980), pp. 146–53. A social systems model for understanding the complex dynamics of intermarriage.

Napier, Augustus, and Carl Whitaker. *The Family Crucible*. New York: Harper & Row, 1977. An amalgam of theory, practice, and case history following the process of family therapy.

Younghusband, Eileen, ed. *Social Casework with Families*. Chicago: University of Chicago Press, 1965. A book of articles by U.S. and English authors describing some kinds of work done in family settings by workers who see themselves as caseworkers.

CHAPTER 6

Cartwright, Dorwin, and Alvin Zander, eds. *Group Dynamics, Research and Theory*. Evanston, Ill.: Row, Peterson, 1953. The bible of group dynamics; a large and comprehensive reference.

Corey, Gerald, and Marianne Corey. *Groups: Process and Practice*. Monterey, Calif.: Brooks/Cole Publishing, 1977. An easily followed account of group process.

Garland, James A.; Hubert Jones; and Ralph Kolodny. "A Model for Stages in the Development of Social Work Groups." In *Explorations of Groupwork*, ed. Saul Berstein. Boston: Boston University Press, 1965. A simple, easily understood model for group development and process.

Hartford, Margaret. *Groups in Social Work*. New York: Columbia University Press, 1972. An application of small-group theory and research to social work practice.

Lewis, Howard, and Harold Sheffield. *Growth Games*. New York: Bantam Books, 1970. Some practical how-to exercises in growth groups.

Northen, Helen. *Social Work with Groups*. New York: Columbia University Press, 1969. A systems-oriented explanation of social group work for the beginning practitioner.

Thomas, Edwin J., ed. *Behavioral Science for Social Workers*. New York: Free Press, 1967. A collection of readings in various areas of social work, including group work.

CHAPTER 7

Brager, George, and Stephen Holloway. *Changing Human Service Organizations: Politics and Practice*. New York: Free Press, 1978. Suggestions for initiating change without high formal power.

Costin, Lela B. "School Social Work as Specialized Practice." *Social Work* 26 (January 1981), pp. 36–40. School social work helps all children, families, and organizations.

Dinerman, Miriam. *Social Work Curriculum at the Baccalaureate and Master's Levels*. New York: The Lois & Samuel Silberman Fund, 1981. An effort to analyze and interpret currently used curricula from a sample of sixty-three different programs in the United States.

Kurzman, Paul, and Sheila Akabe. "Industrial Social Work as an Arena for Practice." *Social Work* 26 (January 1981), pp. 52–59. A plea for social work in industry.

Miringoff, Marc L. *Management in Human Service Organizations*. New York: Macmillan, 1980. A comprehensive approach to managing a variety of programs.

Randolph, Terry, and James Taylor. "Short-changed in the Job Market: A Shopper's Guide." *Social Casework* 60 (December 1979), pp. 616–19.

Sari, Rosemary, and Yeheskel Hasenfield. *The Management of Human Services*. New York: Columbia University Press, 1978.

Scurfield, Raymond. "Clinician to Administrator: Difficult Role Transition." *Social Work* 26 (November 1981), pp. 495–500.

CHAPTER 8

Brownlee, Ann Tampleton. *Community, Culture, and Care*. St. Louis: C. V. Mosby, 1978. A how-to book for community health care.

Clark, Kenneth. *Dark Ghetto: Dilemmas of Social Power*. New York: Harper & Row, 1965. The view of power from a black perspective.

Cox, Fred, et al. *Strategies of Community Organization*. Itasca, Ill.: F. E. Peacock Publishers, 1970. A book of readings discussing definitions, variations, strategies, and linkages.

Dunham, Arthur. *Community Welfare Organization, Principles and Practice*. New York: Thomas Y. Crowell, 1958. A traditional explanation of locality development as viewed by early community workers.

Kramer, Ralph, and Harry Specht. *Readings in Community Organization Practice*. Englewood Cliffs, N.J.: Prentice-Hall, 1969. A book of readings discussing the context and process of community work in terms of analysis, problem solving, roles and social planning.

London, Joan, and Henry Anderson. *So Shall You Reap*. New York: Thomas Y. Crowell, 1970. The story of Cesar Chavez and the farm workers' movement.

Ross, Murray. *Case Histories in Community Organization*. New York: Harper & Row, 1958. A casebook of community organization problems, with questions to be answered at the end of each chapter.

Shaffer, Anatole. "Community Organization and the Oppressed." *Journal of Education for Social Work* 8 (Fall 1972), p. 65. An article explaining the dilemma of working for the oppressed while a member of the oppressor group.

CHAPTER 9

Allen, Josephine A., and N. Yolanda Burwell. "Ageism and Racism: Two Issues in Social Work Education and Practice." *Journal for Social Work Education*, Spring 1981, pp. 71–77. The combination of ageism and racism needs attention from professionals.

Brieland, Donald, et al. *Contemporary Social Work*. New York: McGraw-Hill, 1980. Chapter 16 deals with racism.

Comer, James P., and Alvin F. Poussaint. *Black Child Care*. New York: Simon & Schuster, 1975. How to bring up a healthy black child in America.

Kumabe, Kazue, et al. *Bridging Ethno-Cultural Diversity in Social Work and Health*. Honolulu: University of Hawaii School of Social Work, 1985.

Lum, Doman. *Social Work Practice with People of Color*. Monterey, Calif.: Brooks/Cole Publishing, 1986. The best practice text available.

Monk, Abraham. "Social Work With the Aged: Principles and Practice." *Social Work* 26 (January 1981), pp. 61–67. Social work can improve and enhance individual functioning.

Young, Leontine. *Wednesday's Children*. New York: McGraw-Hill, 1964. A study of child neglect and abuse.

CHAPTER 10

Kincaid, J. C. *Poverty and Equality in Britain*. Middlesex, England: Penguin Books, 1973. A book exploding the theory that Britain has solved the poverty problem.

Turner, Joanne C., and Francis J. Turner, eds. *Canadian Social Welfare*. 2nd ed. Don Mills, Ontario: Collier Macmillan Canada, 1986.

Yelaja, Shankar A., ed. *An Introduction to Social Work Practice in Canada*. Scarborough, Ontario: Prentice-Hall Canada Inc., 1985.

INDEX

Abbott, Edith, 189
Abbott, Grace, 189
Abramovitz, Mimi, 170
Acceptance, 11, 13
Ackerman, Nathan, 9, 82, 193
Addams, Jane, 38, 189
Adler, Alfred, 43
Administrator, 28
Adolescent, 80, 141
Advocate, 28
AFDC, 3, 10, 63, 113, 149
Africa, slaves from, 36
Agency, welfare, 26, 43, 53, 54, 55, 109
Alanon, 103
Alcoholics, 54
Alcoholics Anonymous, 103
Alinsky, Saul, 126, 145–46
Allen, Josephine, 196
Almshouse, 36, 155
Ambrosino, Salvatore, 193
American Psychiatric Association, 144
American Red Cross, 46, 112
Anal stage, 80
Anderson, Henry, 195
Apte, Robert, 190

Baccalaureate degree, 177
Baer, Betty, 8, 15, 177
Bakalinsky, Rosalie, 114
Baltimore, Charity Organization Society of, 42
Barnett, Henrietta, 50
Barnett, Samuel, 38
Bartlett, Harriet M., 7, 15, 189
Beck, Bertram, 174
Beers, Clifford, 50
Begging, 32
Behavior: changer, 28; modification, 71, 72
Behaviorist, 70
Bell, Daniel, 171

Benne, Kenneth D., 190
Bennis, Warren G., 190
Berrien, T. Kenneth, 191
Biestek, Felix, 9, 55
Billingsley, Andrew, 36–37, 50, 141, 193
Blum, Arthur, 91
Boehm, Werner, 47, 50
Booth, Charles, 37, 50
Borenzweig, Harman, 115
Boszeomenyi-Nagy, Ivan, 81
Boulding, Kenneth, 191
Boundaries, 19
Bowen, Murray, 74, 79
Boy Scouts, 89
Boy with a Knife, 96
Brace, Charles Loring, 41
Bracy, John J., 193
Brager, George, 13, 194
Branmer, Laurence, 192
Breckenridge, Sophonisba, 189
Brieland, Donald, 150, 196
British Association of Social Workers, 164
Broker, 28
Brown, Dee, 150
Brownlee, Ann, 195
Bruce, Maurice, 191
Bryant, Anita, 144
Buffalo, New York, 41
Bureaucracy, 109, 110
Burton, John, 164
Burwell, N. Yolanda, 196

Canada, 35, 109, 145, 153–54, 159, 165, 171
Canadian government, 146
Care giver, 28
Carter, Jimmy, 48
Cartwright, Darwin, 96, 194
Cases: acceptance, 11; behavior modification, 71; community, 123, 126–27; contract, 60;

i

Cases—*Cont.*
  diagnostic, 67; expression of feeling, 10;
  family, 76, 78, 81; functional, 68; group, 102;
  individualization, 100; interview, 57;
  involvement, 11; nonjudgmental attitude,
  11; planned change, 25; reality therapy, 69;
  roles, 27; self-determination, 12; social
  work system, 18; termination, 61
Casework: defined, 53; and Mary Richmond,
  42; process, 54; relationship, 9; seven
  principles, 12–13; skills, 8
Caseworkers, 9
Caucasian, 140, 146
Cause and effect, 21
CETA, 171
Chalmers, Thomas, 40
Chamber of Commerce, 197
Change: agent, 27; in English system, 34;
  initiation of, 26; models in casework, 66;
  planned, 42; process, 25–26
Charity, 39
Charity Organization Society, 39–40
Chicano, 77, 139
Child laborers, 34
Children's Aid Society of New York, 41
Children's Home Society, 111
Chin, Robert, 190
Christianity, 32
Chrysler Corporation, 4
Citizens Aid, 156, 159
Clark, Kenneth, 195
Classical, 70
Client participation, 22, 70
Clockwork Orange, 71
Code of ethics, 14; NASW Code of Ethics,
  175
Cohen, Ruth, 192
Collins, Alice H., 189
Comer, James P., 196
Communication, 84, 143
Communicative-integrative approach, 83
Communism, 153
Community, 23, 119–35
Community action programs, 48, 135
Community chests, 134
Community councils, 134
Community planner, 28, 129, 133; community
  work, 119, 133, 135; history, 120
Compton, Beulah, 48, 50, 191
Confidentiality, 12–13
Conflict, 19, 127, 129
Congressional Research Report, 149
Conjoint family therapy, 83
Connectives, 20
Conservative party, 156

Consultant, 28
Contract, 58
Controlled emotional involvement, 11
Copp, Owen, 50
Corey, Gerald, 194
Costin, Lela, 148, 194
Council on Social Work Education, 47, 118
Cow as a system, 17
Cox, Fred, 195
Coyle, Grace, 90
Crampton, Helen M., 49, 189
Cuban American, 139–40

Data manager, 28
Delinquency, juvenile, 6, 21
Dennison, Edward, 37
Depression, 44–46
Developmental system, 20
Development, human, 20; disability, 126,
  141
Diagnostic school, 67
Dickens, Charles, 35
Dinerman, Miriam, 195
Dolgoff, Ralph, 191
Dunham, Arthur, 195

Eckerd Foundation, 104, 112
Ecklein, Joan, 125, 136
Economics, 34, 165
Economic Security Bill (1935), 45
Education, social work, 47, 117–18
Edwards, Tommy, 181
Egan, Gerard, 101, 192
Ego, 80
Elizabethan Poor Law, 33, 109; refine-
  ments of, 34–35
Encyclopedia of Social Work, 7, 104, 151
Enders, Lisa, 182
Engerman, Stanley, 50
England, 32, 34, 37
Environment as explanation of behavior, 22–23
Epstein, Irvin, 190
Epstein, Laura, 72
Erikson, Erik, 67
Evaluation, 64
Evaluator, 28

Face to Face, 101
Families, 149; black, 149
Family, 7, 17, 74; alternatives to, 75; black
  matriarchal, 77; Chicano, 77; defined, 74;
  roles, 73; as a system, 74; therapy, 79,
  85; workers, 9

Family service, 57
Family therapy, 76, 79–80; communicative-
    interactive approach, 82; conjoint, 83; in-
    tegrative approach, 83; psychoanalytic
    approach, 80–81
Farm Security Administration, 45
Farm Workers Union, 133
Federal Emergency Administration, 45
Fedrico, Ron, 117, 191
Feedback, 19–20, 22, 24
Feeling, expression of, 10, 13
Feldstein, Donald, 191
Fellin, Philip, 190
Feminization of poverty, 149
Fendrich, James, 171
Fink, Arthur, 190
Fogel, Robert, 50
Food stamps, 3, 110, 149
"43 Elizabeth," 33, 121
Fox, Evelyn, 192
Framo, James L., 81
France, 33
Freedom riders, 163
Freudian, 80, 153
Freud, Sigmund, 7, 43
Friedlander, Walter, 190
Friendship group, 185
Functional school, 67

Garland, James A., 194
Garrett, Annette, 192
Giovannini, Jeanne, 50, 141, 193
Girl Scouts, 89
Glasser, William, 69
Goddard, H.H., 15
Gordon, William E., 190
Gramm, Rudman Hollings Act, 168
Great Britain, 109, 153–55, 159
Great Society, 48
Grosser, Charles, 132
Group: defined, 23, 87; encounter, 9, 102;
    growth, 100; home, 102; primary, 88;
    sensitivity, 102; small, 23, 88; stages, 85; task,
    101; techniques, 96; training, 102
Group workers, 9, 43, 65, 95

Haley, Alex, 150
Haley, Jay, 74, 85
Harmon, Willis, 171
Harrington, Michael, 190
Hartford, Margaret, 194
Hartman, Ann, 191, 193
Head Start, 48
Health Maintenance Organization, 162

Hearn, Gordon, 191
Henry VIII, 32
Heredity, as explanation of behavior, 22
Hill, Octavia, 40
History of social work, 31–49
Hoffman, Lynn, 85
Hollis, Florence, 15, 59, 68
Homosexual, 140, 145–44, 164
Homeostasis, family, 83
Hoover, Herbert, 44
Hopkins, Harry, 171
Hospital as a system, 24
Howard, Donald, 13, 15
Hull House, 38
Human development, 7, 21

Identified patient, 85
Independent Sector, 169
Idigenous worker, 134
Individualization, 10
Individuals, 21
Initiation of change, 26
Input, 19, 25; social work, 18–19
Institutional concepts, 3
Institutional racism, 7, 65, 148–49
Insurance, social, 45
Integrative approach to family therapy, 82
Intelligence quotient, 22
Interdependent, 25
International Code of Ethics, 177
International social work, 151–59
Intersystem, 20, 24
Interview, 56–57
Involvement, controlled emotional, 11, 56

Jackson, Don, 9, 84
Janchill, Sister Mary Paul, 191
Johnson, Lyndon B., 47, 150
Johnson, H. Wayne, 190
Johnson, Louise, 190
Jung, Carl, 43
Juvenile court, 26, 66
Juvenile delinquency, 6, 21

Kadushin, Alfred, 56, 192
Kahn, Alfred, 152, 158-60
Kaiser, Kenneth K., 49
Kammerman, Sheila, 152, 158–60
Kaufman, Irvin, 192
Kent, Marilyn, 193
Kennedy, John F., 47
Kincaid, J.C., 196
King, Martin Luther, 130

Klenk, Robert W., 190
Knowledge, skills, values, 7
Konopka, Gisela, 90–91
Kramer, Ralph, 195
Kumahe, Kazuge, 196
Kurzman, Paul, 195

L'Abate, Luciano, 85
Labour party, 156
Ladies of Charity, 33
Lauffer, Armand, 125, 136
Leader, Arthur L., 83
Lebeaux, Charles N., 3–4
Legal aid, 48
Lesbian, 141
Lesser eligibility, 34
Lewin, Kurt, 102
Lewis, Howard, 194
Libido, 80
Lind, Roger, 190
Lippitt, Ronald, 27
Locality development, 122, 133
Local responsibility, 32, 40
Loch, Charles, 40
Lockheed Company, 4
London, Joan, 195
London society, 41
Lowenstein, Sidney, 114
Lum, Doman, 196

McPheeters, Harold L., 27
Macrosystems, 107
Marriage counseling, 143
Master's degree, 117
Means test, 41, 45; tested, 4
Mediating worker, 66
Mediator, 93
Medicaid, 3
Medical social worker, 8
Medicare, 3
Mental health, 25
Mental Health Association, 124
Mexican Americans, 140–42
Meyer, Carol, 169–70
Middle ages, 32
Midtown Manhattan Study of Mental Health, 25
Migrants, 127
Miller, Henry, 117, 190
Miller, Sherod, 193
Minihan, Anne, 73
Minorities, 8, 139
Miringoff, Marc, 195
Mobilizer, 28

Monk, Abraham, 196
Montiel, Miguel, 77
Morales, Armondo, 142, 150
Moral majority, 165

Napier, Augustus, 193
NASW Code of Ethics, 175
National Association of Manufacturers, 146
National Association of Social Workers, 14, 116–17, 140, 167, 170–171
National Conference on Charities and Corrections, 43
National health, 156
National Institute of Health, 79
National Youth Administration, 45
Native American, 139, 142, 145
Neurosis, 81
Nixon, Richard, 48
Noble, Kenneth, 146
Nonjudgmental attitude, 11, 13
Northen, Helen, 194

Oedipal stage, 80
Olmsted, Michael, 23, 88
Operant conditioning, 70
Oral, 80
Oriental, 140
Outdoor relief, 41
Output, 16–17, 19, 21
Outreach, 27, 29
Oxley, Genevieve, 193

Papell, Catherine, 88, 90, 92–94
Parents Anonymous, 103
Parsons, Talcott, 191
Participation, client, 22, 70
Pauper's oath, 41
Pavlov, Ivan, 70
Peace Corps, 123, 129–30
Pearl Harbor, 46
Pentagon, 163
Perception of need for change, 27
Perlman, Helen H., 15, 53, 55, 68
Philadelphia Society for Organizing Charity, 42
Philanthropy, 35
Pincus, Allen, 73
Planned change, 25–26, 54, 58, 63, 128; achieving a terminal relationship, 27; establishing a relationship, 26; generalization and stabilization, 27; initiating, 27; perception of need, 27; phases of, 26–27; working toward, 27
Planner, 125, 129

Plebescite, 158
Political system, 17
Politics, 14, 31, 165
Pollack, Otto, 82
Poor: power of, 35; worthy and unworthy, 35
Poor law (1601), 33–34
Poussaint, Alvin, 196
Power, 35
Private practice, 114
Privatization, 170
Process, 26
Proposition 13, 167
Psychiatric social worker, 6, 8
Psychiatrists, 79
Psychoanalytic approach, 80–81
Psychologists, 79, 84, 87
Public welfare, 3–5
Purposeful expression of feeling, 10, 13
Puerto Rican, 139–40

Quaranta, Mary Ann, 170
Questionnaire, 6

Racism, 8
Randolph, Tony, 195
Rank, Otto, 43
Rausch, Julia, 150
Reagan, Ronald, 48, 147, 167, 170
Reality therapy, 69–70
Reciprocal model, 93
Red Cross, 4, 78, 113
Redl, Fritz, 91
Regional Rehabilitation Research Institute, 79
Reid, William, 72
Relationship: interpersonal, 164; in systems, 19
Relief, 34, 36
Religion: and change, 162; and the future, 163; and social work history, 31
Remedial model, 91, 95
Residual concept, 3–4
Respondent conditioning, 70
Richmond, Mary, 42–43, 50
Roles of social workers, 27
Roosevelt, Franklin D., 44–45
Rosenbaum, David, 166
Ross, Murray, 119, 195
Rothman, Beulah, 88, 90, 92–94
Rothman, Jack, 121
Russell Sage Foundation, 42
Ryan, Robert, 27, 190

St. Angelo, Douglas, 171
St. Botolph's, Aldgate, 155

St. Vincent DePaul, 33
Sari, Rosemary, 195
Satir, Virginia, 9, 15, 84
Schenk, Quentin, 192
Schizophrenic, 79
School social worker, 7, 114
Schulman, Eveline, 190
Schwartz, William, 58, 60, 65, 83, 93–94
Scientific method, 39, 49
Scurfield, Raymond, 195
Self-awareness, 14
Self-determination, 12, 71
Settlement: movement, 38; house, 123
Settlement, Act of 1662, 34
Shaffer, Anatole, 196
Sheafor, Bradford, 142, 150
Sheehan, Susan, 190
Shubert, Margaret, 193
Shulman, Lawrence, 60, 95, 98–99
Single parents, 111
Sisters of Charity, 33
Situation and casework, 59
Skills, 7, 8
Skinner, B.F., 70
Slavery, 36–37
Smalley, Ruth, 193
Small groups, 23
Social action, 126, 130, 133
Social casework: change models, 69–72; definitions, 53
Social diagnosis, 42
Social goals model, 88, 90
Social insurance, 45; old age, 162
Social planning, 125
Social Security Act (1935), 4, 45, 51; laws, 161
Social services in international perspective, 152
Social systems, 1; boundaries, 19; conflict, 19; connectives, 20; defined, 16; developmental, 20; equilibrium, 20; intersystem, 20; tension, 19; strain, 19; stress, 19; terms, 19–20
Social welfare, 3–5, 161, 163
Social work: defined, 17; intercultural aspects, 153; skills, 8; values, 9, 161
Social work education, 47; 117–18, 151
Social work future, 161–73
Social work history, 31–49; systems affecting, 31
Social work system, 18
Social work with families, 74
Sociologists, 79, 87
Spaceship Earth, 17
Specht, Harry, 121, 195
Srole, Leo, 25
State and local responsibility, 40

Stockman, David, 171
Strain, 19
Stress, 19
Superego, 80
Switzerland, 153, 157–59
Symbiosis, 93
Symbiotic, 61
System: defined, 16–20; developmental, 20–22, 25; diagrammed, 24; interrelationships of, 19; personal, 22; political, 17; social work, 18; solar, 17; subsystem, 21, 123, 161; terms, 19
Szasz, Thomas, 193

T groups, 102–3; training groups, 102–4
Task groups, 100
Tasks of social work, five central, 58–59, 65, 83, 95
Taxes, 5
Teacher, 28
Tension, 19
Terman, Lewis M., 22
Termination, 27, 62–64, 130–31
Thomas, Edwin J., 194
Titmuss, Richard, 5
Toynbee Hall, 38
Trattner, Walter, 192
Tripodi, Tony, 190
Tropp, Emmamuel, 104
Truly needy, 49
Turner, Francis J., 66

Unemployment, 44, 157–58, 166, 169; insurance, 157–58, 162
United Nations, 151
United Service Organization, 46

University of Washington, 80
Urban Institute, 168

Vagrancy, 32
Values, 9–13, 142
Veterans Administration, 5
Victorians, 37, 49
Vinter, Robert, 91–92
Vista, 48
Voluntarism, 109, 112
Voluntary agencies, 111–12
Volunteers, 130–31, 134
Von Bertalanffy, Ludwig, 176, 191

Warren, Roland, 119
Washington, University of, 80
Watson, James, 27
Webb, Beatrice Potter, 37, 39
Welfare, connotations, 3–5, 10, 13
Welfare Mothers Speak Out, 113
Welfare state, 45, 153, 170
Western thought, 31
Westley, Bruce, 27
Wilensky, Harold, 3–4, 15
Wilson, Gertrude, 90, 100
Whitaker, Carl, 194
Woodroofe, Kathleen, 35, 49
Workhouse Act of 1696, 33
Works Progress Administration, 45

Yalom, Irwin D., 101
YMCA, 90
Young, Leontine, 196
Younghusband, Eileen, 153, 160, 194

Zander, Alvin, 96, 179, 194
Zastrow, Charles, 192

ABOUT THE AUTHOR

Betty Piccard was born in St. Paul, Minnesota. She received the Bachelor of Arts degree with a major in sociology, cum laude, and the Master of Arts in Social Work from the University of Minnesota. She also served in the U.S. Navy, W.A.V.E.S. Since 1969, Professor Piccard has taught graduate and undergraduate social work students at Florida State University. Twice she has taught on the Florida State System London Program. In 1975, she was appointed Director of the Undergraduate Program in Social Work, her primary responsibility for the past thirteen years. She has held social work positions with Travelers Aid, the American Red Cross, the Girl Scouts, and the Mental Health Association. She is married and the mother of five grown children.

A Note on the Type

The text of this book was set in 10/13 Palatino using a film version of the face designed by Hermann Zapf that was first released in 1950 by Germany's Stempel Foundry. The face is named after Giovanni Battista Palatino, a famous penman of the 16th century. In its calligraphic quality, Palatino is reminiscent of the Italian Renaissance type designs, yet with its wide, open letters and unique proportions it still retains a modern feel. Palatino is considered one of the most important faces from one of Europe's most influential type designers.

Composed by Eastern Graphics, Binghamton, New York.

Printed and bound by Malloy Lithographing, Inc., Ann Arbor, Michigan.